The Feelings Book

The Care & Keeping of Your Emotions

by Dr. Lynda Madison
illustrated by Josée Masse

★ American Girl®

*I get mad a lot at little things that happen.
I don't show that I'm upset, but in my room I cry.
I try to tell my family about it, but either they
don't listen or telling them makes it worse.
I don't know what to do.*
Feeling Angry

Published by American Girl Publishing
Copyright © 2002, 2013 by American Girl

This book is not intended to replace the advice or treatment of
health-care professionals. It should be considered an additional
resource only. Questions and concerns about mental or physical
health should always be discussed with a doctor or other health-
care professional.

Questions or comments? Call 1-800-845-0005,
visit **americangirl.com**, or write to Customer Service,
American Girl, 8400 Fairway Place, Middleton, WI 53562-0497.

Printed in China
13 14 15 16 17 18 19 20 LEO 10 9 8 7 6 5 4 3 2 1

All American Girl marks are trademarks of American Girl.

Editorial Development: Michelle Watkins, Therese Kauchak,
Carrie Anton, Barbara Stretchberry
Art Direction and Design: Chris Lorette David, Camela DeCaire
Production: Judith Lary, Paula Moon, Tami Kepler, Kristi Tabrizi
Illustrations: Josée Masse

A Letter to You

When you were little, **your emotions were simple.** You smiled when you were happy. You cried when you were scared or hurt. You had only a few ways of responding to what happened to you, and you didn't think about your moods much at all.

Now that you're older, your emotions are more complicated. You might freeze up during a test or slam your door when you're mad. It might seem like you're on an **emotional roller coaster**—up one minute and down the next. But if you learn more about your feelings, you can keep them from racing out of control. You can be in charge—and that makes the ride a whole lot easier.

Table of Contents

How Do You Feel?

How do you feel at this very moment? **Happy? Sad? Angry? Scared?** Lots of things in your life can set off your emotions. Sometimes you will feel good . . . sometimes not so good. But all those feelings—the good, the sad, and the all-around bad—are normal. And chances are, even the happiest girl you know is sorting out her own confusing knot of emotions. So hold on and hang in there, and we'll help you figure this feelings thing out.

What Are Feelings?

"I feel great!" "I feel mad." "I feel scared!" Just what are these oceans of emotions washing over you these days?

Emotions are reactions you have to things that happen around you, and you use "feeling" words to describe them. Because the events you react to are constantly changing, it's natural that your emotions would change, too! (That's why the word "emotion" has the word "motion" built right into it.) You can be soaring to the top of the world one minute and feel stuck in the mud the next. Sometimes you may not even be sure how you feel at all.

Some days I feel happy one minute and like crying the next. I continually get mad when people ask me about my day, and I often blow up at my mom. What is happening? Why do I do this?
Confused

The better you become at identifying your feelings, the more you'll learn about yourself. People often use the words on the facing page to describe their feelings. Circle any feelings you remember having in the last week.

I felt . . .

thrilled

proud

shy

fearful

honored

guilty

wonderful

happy

ashamed

anxious

joyful

scared

confused

frustrated

envious

sad

annoyed

ambitious

excited

moody

embarrassed

pleased

serious

compassionate

worried

silly

brave

hopeless

sorry

loving

hopeful

giddy

respectful

careless

Your Mood-O-Meters

Each feeling you have can be strong, mild, or somewhere in between. For each situation, fill in the mood-o-meter to show where your feelings would register. If you have feelings that aren't listed here, create a new mood-o-meter.

1. You're doing homework on the computer and you accidentally delete your whole file. You feel

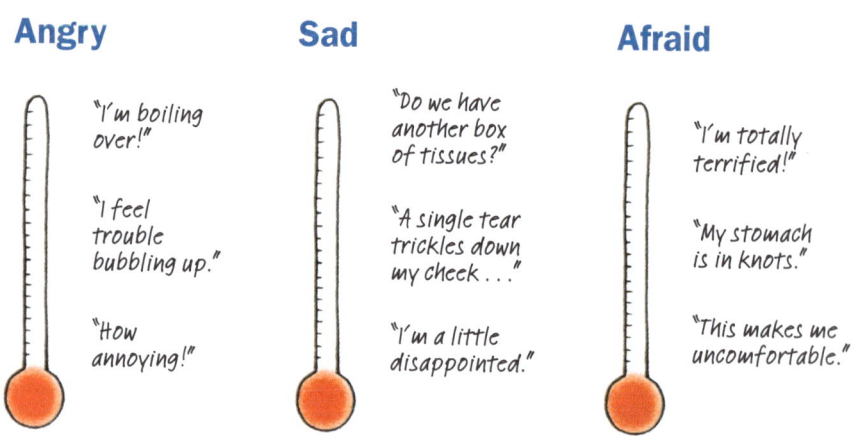

Angry

"I'm boiling over!"

"I feel trouble bubbling up."

"How annoying!"

Sad

"Do we have another box of tissues?"

"A single tear trickles down my cheek . . ."

"I'm a little disappointed."

Afraid

"I'm totally terrified!"

"My stomach is in knots."

"This makes me uncomfortable."

2. Mom announces that your family will be spending the entire summer at the beach. You feel

Happy

"Look out, ocean, here I come!"

"I'm getting excited . . ."

"I'm oh-so-satisfied."

Angry

"N–O. I won't go! N–O. I won't go!"

"Argh! I told my friends I'd sign up for summer soccer!"

"But I won't know anyone there."

Sad

"I'd call this 'super-sob sad.' "

"I'm getting teary!"

"But I'll miss my room at home."

3. Someone says a friend is spreading a nasty rumor about you. You feel

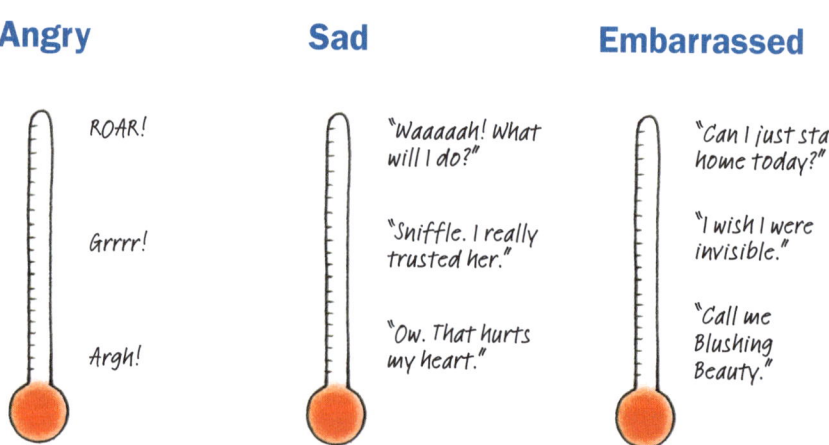

Angry

ROAR!

Grrrr!

Argh!

Sad

"Waaaaah! What will I do?"

"Sniffle. I really trusted her."

"Ow. That hurts my heart."

Embarrassed

"Can I just stay home today?"

"I wish I were invisible."

"Call me Blushing Beauty."

4. You walk onto the stage to sing your solo, and you trip over the top step. You feel

Angry

"That's it! I quit!"

"Someone should have told me about that step! Who's in charge around here?"

"I knew I should have practiced my entrance."

Sad

"I can't sing when I'm crying!!"

"The reviews will call this an emotional performance."

"I wish I hadn't blown my big chance."

Embarrassed

"I wish this was a disappearing act!"

"If I trip on the way back out, maybe it will look like part of the act."

"Sheesh. I hope no one saw that!"

If you marked several mood-o-meters for any situation, congratulations! It's normal to feel more than one emotion at a time. If you weren't sure where to mark the mood-o-meters, you might not easily be flustered by your feelings. If you knew for sure, you might react strongly to some things that happen around you. But don't worry—you're going to learn how to keep feelings from boiling over.

The Brain, the Body & Butterflies

When something happens around you or to you, **your brain receives the message and tells your body systems how to react**—sometimes before you even realize it. (That's where those butterflies in your stomach come from.) Your brain works with the rest of your body as a team to help you deal with your emotions.

Brain Power

Your brain takes your feelings and makes them physical.

Your brain is in charge of everything you do, from your breathing to how you feel at any point in time. Things like movies or bad dreams aren't exciting or scary unless your brain decides they are. It gets input from everything you see, hear, feel, taste, and smell, and it responds quickly to tell your body how to react.

When I get blamed for things my little sister does, it makes me so mad that I burst into tears! After a while I cool off. Then I sit down with my parents and talk about what happened, and usually someone apologizes.
Marta, Oregon

In fact, just about every emotion you have is connected to some reaction in your body. You may blush when you're embarrassed, cry when you're sad, and jump when you're startled.

Sweaty Palms and Knocking Knees

When other parts of your body get the message that your brain is sending, they **burst into action!**

Tightening Up

When you feel tense, your muscles can get tight. You might clench your teeth, hunch up your shoulders, squint your eyes, or hold your hands in tight fists.

Feeling Butterflies

When you are stressed, your body produces chemicals that can make you feel shaky or weak. It may feel like someone is using your stomach for a trampoline. Some people call this "having the jitters" or "having butterflies in your stomach."

Sweating It

When your emotions run strong, your forehead, armpits, hands—even the insides of your elbows—might sweat.

Knocking Knees

When you get nervous, your kneecaps may bounce up and down, especially if you're standing up. When you sit, your whole leg might bounce!

Blushing Beauty

You may get red in the face when your moods run high, especially if you're fair-skinned. But anyone's face can feel hot in reaction to strong emotions, even if it doesn't turn a few shades of red.

Ka-THUMP! Ka-THUMP!

Has your heart ever beaten so hard and fast, you thought the whole class would hear it? Strong emotions can even make you feel as though your heart were climbing up into your throat.

Casting a Dizzy Spell

Breathing too quickly can pump too much oxygen to your brain. Not breathing often enough can pump too little. Either one can leave you feeling dizzy or faint.

When you experience one of these physical reactions, don't freak out. It's normal. And it shouldn't stop you from trying new things, whether you're giving a speech, dancing in public, or saying hi to that new girl in class (imagine the emotions she must be feeling!).

Fight or Flight?

When you're upset, your heart beats faster and you start breathing more quickly. It's **your body's way of responding** to protect you.

That thumping heart is part of your body's "fight-or-flight" reaction, and it goes back to when humans first walked the earth.

Suppose you were a cave girl, just hanging out one day with your cave friends, when a fierce and hungry cave bear charged into camp. Your body's automatic responses would help you either tangle with the bear (fight) or run for your life (take flight). If you didn't do one or the other, you'd probably get eaten.

In order to fight or run away, your body would need to pump more blood to your heart (thus the pounding feeling). It would need to get your legs ready to run (thus the tight muscles). Your breathing might slow down at first so that you could be quiet and size up the situation. Then you'd probably breathe faster than normal, supplying extra oxygen to your body. You might sweat and get goose bumps in order to keep cool.

You can have a fight-or-flight reaction even when there isn't any serious danger, such as when you have to give a speech or when you hear bad news. Your body may react the same way you would have reacted as a cave girl, even though no hungry bear is sizing you up for lunch.

Why Do You Cry?

Ever laugh till your sides split? Watch a sad movie? Goof up badly on your history test? **There's a reason** any of these things can leave you in tears.

Crying is an outward sign that you feel strongly about something—usually not getting something you want or getting something you don't want. Everybody cries, even grown-ups and boys. Sometimes those tears just have to roll.

Tears serve a purpose. When you cry because of your emotions (not because of chopped onions), your tears release certain chemicals in your body. Scientists think these chemicals might actually make you feel better.

When I'm sad, I cry. Crying is a way to express your feelings. You feel better after it's all over. I also talk out loud to myself so the sadness doesn't stay as a lump in my stomach. **Katherine, Michigan**

So it's OK to cry. Honest. Crying is a normal reaction to strong emotions. But some people cry so often that it becomes a problem. They get their feelings hurt easily and may think others don't like them.

Crying shouldn't replace talking about your feelings or taking actions that might help a situation. Tears just aren't the same as words. If you want people to understand what you are feeling or to know how to help, take a few deep breaths— and start talking.

Feeling Out of Control

Sometimes, before you even know what's going on, you can find yourself feeling angry, weepy, or tingly with excitement. That's parts of your body responding to your **brain releasing hormones.**

Yikes! Sometimes it seems as if you can't control your feelings. That's because feelings are often instantaneous reactions caused by your brain triggering chemicals called *hormones* that course through your body.

The *amygdala* (ah-mig-duh-luh) is a small part of your brain that scientists think is responsible for the way you feel. These two little almond-shaped groups of cells react automatically to situations that your brain thinks are funny, sad, or disturbing in some way, such as someone jumping out at you in the dark or a balloon popping. Whether you're laughing or crying at a movie or screaming as you go down a log ride at an amusement park, your amygdala is hard at work.

The *pituitary* (pi-too-i-tare-ee) is a tiny, pea-sized gland in your brain that releases hormones. Some hormones cause you to grow, while others are responsible for the changes maturing girls go through, such as starting their periods.

I've been feeling a wave of emotions lately, and I can't control it. Last week I felt grouchy and angry for no reason. But this week I've been crying a lot, even when I'm not sad. I've never felt this way before, and it's scaring me.
What's Happening Here?

As your body changes during puberty, these hormones will also start to affect how you feel emotionally. *Premenstrual syndrome* (PMS) is a group of emotional and physical symptoms that some girls—and women—experience a few days to a few weeks before their menstrual period begins each month. Hormonal changes can give you PMS and make you feel irritated or cry more easily. They can also cause headaches, tiredness, backaches, or sore breasts. Not every girl experiences PMS, and these feelings usually decrease or disappear within the first two days of your period.

What Can You Do?

The good news is that your amygdala and hormones don't act on their own. **There are lots of things you can do** to feel more in charge of your feelings.

Another part of your brain, the *cerebrum* (ser-ee-brum), works with the amygdala to help you manage your emotions. The cerebrum is the thinking part of your brain. Whereas the amygdala sounds the alarm, the cerebrum takes time to help you decide what to do. When you feel stressed out, let your cerebrum kick in. Try these exercises to help yourself relax and stay focused.

Take Three

You need the oxygen in the air you breathe. When you feel anxious, take a long, slow breath through your nose. Count to three as you breathe in, then hold your breath to the count of three. Now breathe out slowly, counting to three again. Repeat this three times and notice how much calmer you feel.

Flex It

When you feel tense, you may tighten your muscles without even noticing. Practice noticing how different muscles feel when they are tense, starting with your feet and moving up to your calves, rear end, back, arms, hands, shoulders, neck, and face. Hold each muscle group tightly to a count of ten, then relax. Imagine you are a pile of wet spaghetti that would just plop onto the plate if someone were to pick it up.

Use Your Imagination

Close your eyes and visualize a favorite calm, relaxing place. Feel as though you are there, with its sights and sounds and smells. Try repeating a lulling phrase to yourself, such as "Seagulls, sand, and surf."

Laugh It Up

Sometimes laughter is the best medicine. Laughing helps the brain make chemicals that stop pain and make you feel good. So laugh at silly things you do, watch a funny movie, or learn a few jokes to get your friends laughing, too.

Move It

Exercise is important for developing strong bones and muscles, and it's a great way to get your mind off things. But jogging, running, or playing a vigorous sport has also been shown to get good chemicals coursing through your brain, which can help you feel better.

Catch the Rhythm

Music can soothe or excite you, depending on its rhythm and its words. Decide what you need, and play songs that will help you relax or distract you from your troubles by getting you humming or dancing along.

Eat Right

Your brain needs the energy that comes from regular, nutritious meals in order to work well and help you solve your problems. Some people don't eat well when they are upset. Other people look to food for comfort, reaching for another cookie when they're upset. But when the cookie's gone, the problem will still be there. People who do this may gain weight and not learn real strategies for solving problems.

Stock Up on Zzzs

Your brain needs sleep to sort through what you've learned during the day and store the information. While snoozing, you're replacing chemicals your brain needs. Nine-year-olds usually need ten hours of sleep per night. Thirteen-year-olds require about nine hours. If you don't sleep enough, you will probably feel tired and grouchy during the day, and then anything that's bothering you is likely to seem even worse than it is.

Gab, Gab, Gab

Call a friend just to chat, or talk to a caring adult about how you are feeling. Sharing your concerns can make you feel better, and sometimes other people have ideas that can help.

Holding It All In

When you feel rotten, it may seem easier just to ignore the bad stuff and hope it all goes away. But a smart girl knows **that's not the way to go.**

When you're really upset, you may be tempted to just lie facedown on your bed and ignore the world. Even doing the things you know will help, such as exercising or talking, may seem like too much work.

But the truth is, keeping your emotions inside—especially the negative ones—only makes you feel worse. Constant stress can even increase your chances of getting sick when colds and flu bugs are going around.

Your mind can suffer, too. The more anxious you get, the more things you notice to be anxious about. You might have trouble making simple decisions, such as what to wear or what homework assignment to do first. You might get cross with people who try to help you, or give up doing things you ordinarily think are fun. The good news: you can get rid of that anxious feeling so that your emotions don't interfere with eating, learning, sleeping, and doing all the other great things waiting out there for you.

How Do You Really Feel?

When your feelings are out of control, you can't think clearly. It's smart to give yourself a chance to dig a little deeper into your emotions. **Thinking things through** helps you avoid doing or saying things you will regret later. It can help other people understand you better. And it can help you find solutions to problems you might think are unsolvable.

What's Your Reaction?

Do you blow up at the drop of a hat, or do you keep your true feelings hidden inside? For each situation, pick the reaction that is closest to the way you would probably respond.

1. You are trying to study. Your brother keeps coming into your room, messing with your games. You aren't getting anything done! You

   a. scream at him to get out—NOW!
   b. call your friend and tell her what a pain he is.
   c. clench your jaw and try to ignore him.

2. Your teacher is passing back tests and pauses at your desk. When you take the paper, a big red mark shows that you failed. You

   a. pound your fist on your desk so loudly that half the class turns around.
   b. check with other kids around you to see how they did.
   c. slide down in your chair and then slink out of class as soon as you can.

3. You open a big white envelope with your name on it and learn you won $100 in a drawing contest! You

    a. jump into the air and let out a whoop!

    b. call all the people you know and tell them the news.

    c. smile to yourself and head straight for the bank.

4. You watch a scary movie after everyone else is in bed, and then see shadowy figures in the closet every time you open your eyes. You

    a. burst out of the bedroom like a ghost is at your heels.

    b. wake your parents and tell them you can't sleep.

    c. lie there shivering for as long as it takes to go to sleep.

Answers

The Nuclear Reactor

If you had mostly **a** answers, you tend to wear your feelings on your sleeve—or anywhere else people can see them. It's great that you don't hold things in, but take care not to react too quickly and shut down communication with another person. If you immediately act angry when, underneath it all, you are actually sad, hurt, or scared, other people will get the wrong impression about how you feel. Pay attention to how your behavior affects others. You might not realize that you say or do thoughtless things that hurt the people around you.

The Talker

If you had mostly **b** answers, you let your feelings out by being chatty. Good—at least they aren't just tumbling around inside of you. Talking to others can help you sort through what you are feeling. But be careful not to speak before you think, or you could say things you regret later. Take time to think about whether you are talking to people who actually want to hear what you have to say, and make sure your words are not hurtful in some way. And don't let your chattiness keep you from figuring out how you really feel.

The Private "I"

If you had mostly **C** answers, you may be great at solving problems by yourself, on your own schedule. Or you might be a very quiet or private person who does not want to burden others with your feelings. This can be fine, as long as you don't have a storm of emotions going on inside. If you do, you'll want to get your feelings out where you can take a good look at them, so that they don't build up to the point that they make you ill. You might want to talk to others about how you feel so that they can offer help if you need it.

Put It in Your Backpack

You may not always be able to deal with your emotions right away. Sometimes it's **OK to let them rest** for a little while until you have time to deal with them.

Suppose a friend says something upsetting to you as you're going into math class, where you're about to take a test. Talking to her during class might help, but it surely would ruin everyone else's concentration. You might feel like crying or even yelling at her, but you'd embarrass yourself—and the teacher might send you to the principal's office. Sometimes you have to wait for a more appropriate time to sort out your feelings.

When we can't deal with our feelings right away, most of us stuff them into an emotional "backpack." It's tempting to leave your feelings in there, especially when your mind has moved on to something else. But if you never think about them again, your backpack could get so full that emotions spill out when you least expect it. Or you could end up carrying around so many emotions that you don't even know what's in your pack anymore. Then your health could suffer, not to mention your moods! One way or another, emotions eventually have to be dealt with.

Tip: Don't wait until bedtime to sort through confusing emotions. You might find it really hard to get some sleep. Try thinking and talking earlier in the evening and tackling just one issue at a time.

Sorting It Out

The feelings that make your backpack the heaviest **aren't always the most obvious** ones.

When you're upset, reach into your backpack and pull out the strongest feeling you're having. Then ask yourself if that's the only emotion in there, or if others are hiding there, too. You run the risk of staying just plain angry if you don't take time to discover what's really bothering you. Try these techniques to get to the bottom of things.

Keep a journal. Writing down your thoughts and feelings every day can help you sort out how you truly feel and help you solve problems. Write as though you are sharing your thoughts with a friend. You might want to keep your journal hidden from the rest of the family, but you should feel free to share it when you want to.

Fill in the blank. If you are having trouble figuring out which emotion you are feeling, try looking at the list of feelings words earlier in this book. Think about the situation that is troubling you, and use each feelings word in this sentence to see if it fits:

"I felt _____ when _____ happened."
     (feeling)   (event)

Talk to someone. Describing the situation can help you decide what you are feeling and can make the solution easier to see. Talking about how you feel may make you anxious or a little shy. Wait until the person can give you his or her full attention, and then say, "Can I talk to you about something I've been feeling lately?" or "Something happened today that I wondered if I could talk to you about. Do you have a minute?"

Make a "Why Else?" list. When someone says or does something that upsets you, try listing other reasons that person might have done what she did. Could she not have known it would hurt your feelings? Could she have been upset about something that didn't have anything to do with you? Her behavior could have more to do with her issues than yours, and making a "why else" list can keep you from jumping to conclusions.

Think of how others have resolved their feelings. Maybe your friend Sarah talked about her sadness and felt better. Maybe Liam hit the teacher and got expelled. Some actions help, but others can make a hard situation even worse.

Talking It Out

Sitting down with someone who cares can make you feel better and help you see your problems in a new light.

Talking to someone about your worries can help you feel less alone. You may open up to Mom or Dad, a friend, an aunt, or your best friend's mother. Whomever you choose, knowing that someone cares about you and wants you to feel better can help lighten your load.

If talking with your friends and family doesn't make you feel better, it is probably time to get professional help. Therapists, psychiatrists, and psychologists talk to you about your emotions and help you solve puzzles about why you feel and act the way you do.

A therapist talks to you (and often your parents) and helps you cope with difficult experiences. A psychiatrist is a doctor who often uses medication to treat mental and emotional disorders. A psychologist is a doctor who helps you learn to change your thoughts and behaviors.

When your thoughts or feelings interfere with the important things in life, getting help is simply the smart thing to do.

The Real World

Katie* has been upset a lot lately. A psychologist helps her understand **what's really bothering her** and what she can do to feel happier.

Katie was angry all the time. Her parents brought her to see a psychologist after she trashed her bedroom in a rage. They all agreed Katie was mad that she had come in second in the gymnastics meet the week before, instead of in her usual first place. Since then, she had been mean to her parents and testy with her sister, and she had failed a quiz in school.

Katie was nervous at first, but after spending a few minutes telling the therapist about herself, she felt a little calmer. Then she started talking about coming in second in her gymnastics meet.

Katie: I am so mad. Those judges are really dumb. I'm a better gymnast than those other girls are. I should have won.

Therapist: Are you angry because you think the judges were wrong?

Katie: Well, I'm not mad at them, I guess. It's just that I usually win.

Therapist: It sounds like you're feeling a little disappointed.

Katie: I guess so. I'm not perfect, you know. I shouldn't always have to get first place in these meets.

Therapist: Someone said you had to get first place?

Katie: Well, no. But my parents act that way. They're so proud and they brag so much when I win.

Therapist: So you think they're disappointed. It sounds like you may feel ashamed because you think you let them down.

Katie: Yes. It's really embarrassing. I'm better than that. They know it, and I know it.

There it was. Katie had acted angry. But actually, she was disappointed, embarrassed, and ashamed that she had let her parents down. Or thought she had.

The interesting thing was, once Katie talked to her parents about how she felt, she discovered they weren't disappointed in her at all! They didn't expect her to be the best all the time. They didn't even realize they were acting differently when she came in second. They were afraid that Katie would be sensitive to her loss and that it would seem insincere if they acted excited about her second-place win. All they really wanted was for her to have a good time—which she did more often once she took the pressure off herself.

*Katie's name and her interests have been changed to protect her privacy.

Strategy Session

Like Katie's feelings, yours may not always be what they seem. When you are emotional about something, **unpack your backpack** and ask the following questions:

How am I telling myself that I feel?

Fill in the blank: "I feel so _____." Your first thoughts about what you are feeling might not be correct. Or that feeling might be only a minor part of what you really feel. There could be other feelings hiding deep in your backpack, way down underneath the one that seems obvious.

Are there other feelings nagging underneath my first emotion—ones I am not even aware of?

Sometimes, underneath that feeling you think is so obvious, you can be feeling afraid, jealous, or sad. Sometimes you want and need attention and are angry when someone else doesn't see that. Take the feelings word you used above and ask yourself, "Why does this situation make me feel _____?"

What else could I be feeling?

See if another feelings word describes your emotions better. Try each one in this sentence: "Could I be feeling a little _____, too?"

Figuring out what is really in your backpack can help you truly understand yourself. Then, if you are feeling blue, you can act in a way that has the best chance of helping you feel better.

The Voice Inside

Ever think about what your thoughts say to you? Sometimes they tell you things about yourself *(I'm a pretty good artist)*, or other people *(I don't think Emma likes me)*, or even what might happen at that party tomorrow *(I don't think anyone is going to talk to me)*. **Some of your thoughts may be true, but others are definitely not.** Learning to understand and train that voice in your head can help you feel strong and confident—and deal with tough times when they come your way.

Listening In

Your inner voice usually chatters away in a pretty calm fashion. But if you're upset, your **thoughts get more emotional** and can make things seem worse than they are.

Positive Voice

When you are happy, proud, excited, or pleased, the messages you give yourself are usually positive.

Things are going really well.

Confident Voice

When you feel good, the voice in your head reminds you of things you like about yourself or of compliments others have given you. These thoughts can give you confidence to try new things and help you do well.

I know this stuff. I'm going to do well on this test.

Upset Voice

When you are sad or disappointed about something, however, your thoughts can get out of control.

I'm a loser— a complete failure.

When you're upset, your thoughts can turn negative and your fears can become exaggerated. Just because you flubbed your social studies test doesn't mean you're dumb. Maybe you were distracted because you stayed up too late last night. Maybe you need a new way to study. When you are angry or sad, that voice in your head may not be telling you the truth. It can call you names and tell you lies. Before you jump to conclusions, remind yourself that your negative voice may be picking up on your fears and making you feel worse.

Understanding the Circle

When you're upset, believing all the negative thoughts whizzing through your brain can make you feel worse. It can even affect how other people treat you.

It's a big circle.

Your emotions affect your thoughts. Your thoughts affect behavior. Your behavior affects other people's reactions. Their reactions affect your emotions!

This is how many of us convince ourselves that the negative voice in our head is right. But when you believe that voice, you can become your own worst enemy. Check out the example on the next page.

Your emotions

Ellie and Leah went to the mall without me. That hurts.

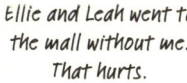

affect **your thoughts about yourself,**

They don't like me anymore. They must be mad at me.

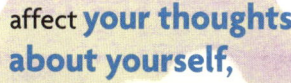

which affects **other people's reactions to your behavior.**

What's up with Alex? She must not want to hang out with us anymore. Let's just ignore her.

which affect **your behavior,**

If they're mad, I'm not going to talk to them. What's the point?

Changing the Circle

Changing your negative thinking can affect how others react to you—and how you feel about what is going on.

Here's how you can change a negative thought:

Stop it short. Catch those negative things you say to yourself, and hit the OFF button. Use a signal to remind yourself: clap your hands, snap a rubber band on your wrist, or even say "Stop" right out loud. Then distract yourself with another activity, such as reading or calling a friend.

Replace it. Think about possible reasons your friends might have acted the way they did. Did they not have time to call you? Did they try to call but couldn't get through? There may be lots of reasons. It's often best just to assume things are fine and go on. Remind yourself that friends can do things separately and still like each other.

Maybe they tried to call when Mom was on the phone.

Check it out. If a negative thought keeps nagging at you, find out if it's really true. Suggest an activity you and your friends can do together. If it still feels as if things aren't right, ask one of your friends privately if she's upset. Do what you can to make things right. Then forgive yourself and them—and remember that you have other friends you can do things with, too, when things are strained.

Clear Away Clouds

You're not the only person whose skies are sometimes darkened by negative thinking. But you can clear away the black clouds by learning to **question those thoughts** and work things through.

"My friend hates me."

Sometimes when you think someone dislikes you, you are actually making up how the other person feels. Before you decide this is true, consider whether something else is going on. Maybe your friend dislikes what you did, but she still likes you. Maybe you were grouchy or unfriendly to her. Talk to her to see if you can learn more. On the other hand, maybe she is worried about her own popularity and is making herself feel better by leaving you out. In that case, consider whether this person is really a good friend.

"I'm not pretty enough."

Worrying about your looks gets you nowhere. Everyone of us can find someone we think is more beautiful than we are. But physical beauty isn't everything. There are great-looking people who are unhappy and average-looking people who are funny, well-liked, and respected. Forget about your reflection and focus on being the best you can be. Be healthy and fit, have fun with your style—and have faith in yourself.

"I'm stupid."

You aren't dumb just because you didn't do your best or as well as someone else did. If you look for things you could have done differently and work at them in the future, you can succeed the next time around. Tell yourself, "This is just one situation in which I didn't do well. I'll work harder next time." Then do it!

Think Smart!

The next time the voice in your head says, "You can't do that," say, **"Yes, I can."** Match a negative thought from the left-hand column with one of the smarter statements on the right. You might find more than one that can help.

59

Who Can You Trust?

Finding someone to talk with can make your feelings easier to deal with—but you have to open up to **the right person.** Read the statements below with a friend in mind to find out how good a listener she is. The more you answer "true," the better she'd be to turn to.

1. Some people seem angry and sad all the time, but not this girl. She is warm and friendly, and not just to you. She doesn't just pretend to be nice.

true   false

2. When she asks how you're doing, she stops what she's doing and actually listens to your answers. She doesn't get distracted by other things.

true   false

3. She never makes fun of other people because of mistakes they've made or tells stories about the dumb things someone else has done. She sticks up for kids whom other people make fun of.

true   false

4. She always follows through on what she says she'll do. When she says she'll call you back, she does.

true   **false**

5. She'd never say a word about anything you told her in private—unless you told her you were going to do something dangerous. Then she'd be sure to get help from an adult.

true   **false**

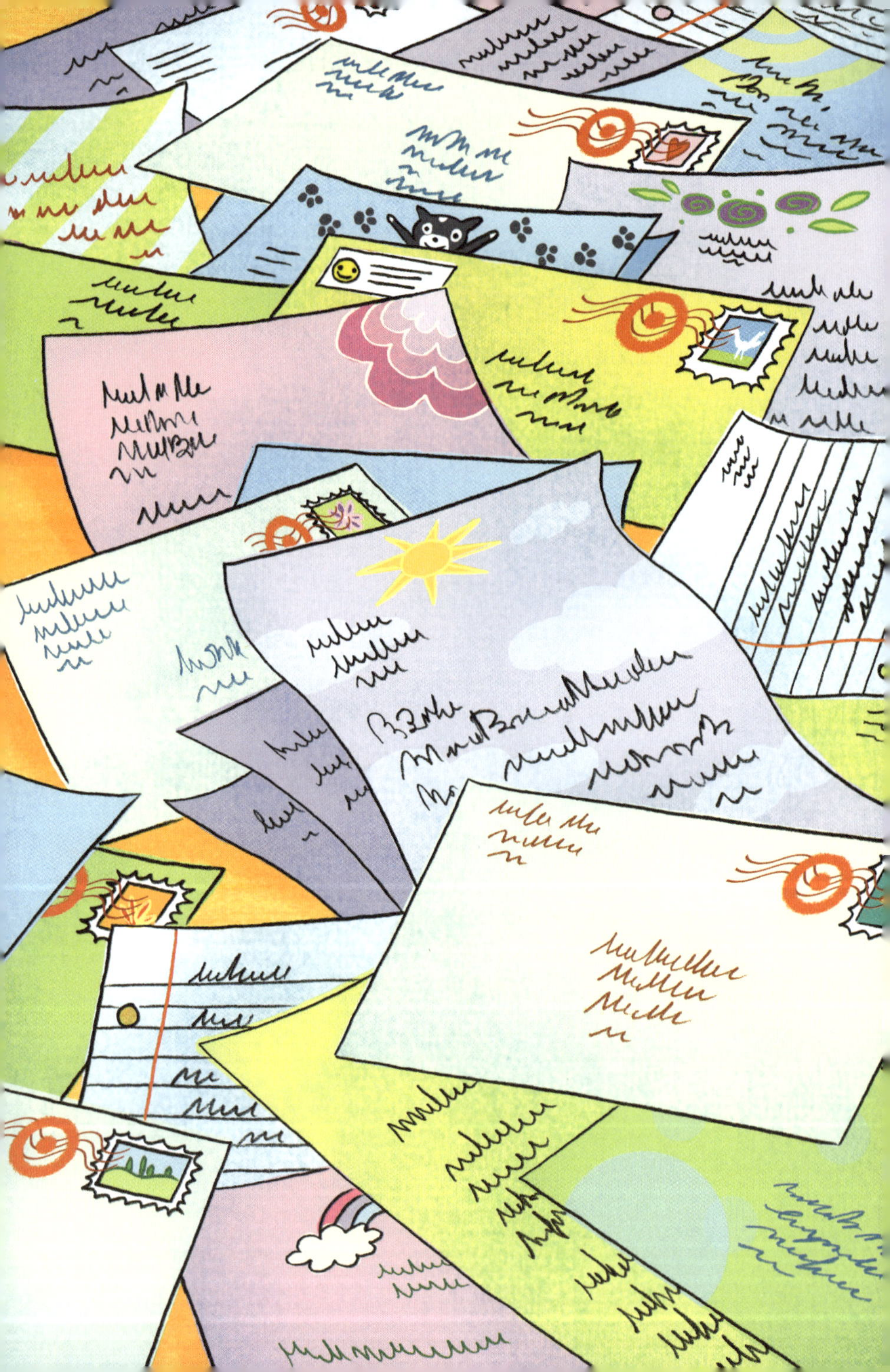

Help!

Lots of girls are dealing with confusing feelings—trying to make sense of them and learning how to cope. The big truth? No matter how you feel, you can always do something to improve a bad situation or to make a good situation better. So even when things happen in your life that you can't change, remember that **you're always in charge** of what you do about the way you feel.

I'm Scared

There are **many types of fear.** Some include the kind you feel at a scary movie, the kind you have when you go down into the dark basement alone, and the kind you feel when you're trying out for the soccer team. What can you do about them?

I am very scared to sleep alone at night. When I'm in bed, I imagine something will come into my room. I really want to be able to sleep alone without being afraid.

Afraid of the Dark

Put your imagination to work calming yourself down. Close your eyes and visualize a bright, cheery place. In your mind, rerun a "film" of something pleasant that happened recently—or create one about something fun coming up in your life.

If you get distracted from your imaginary movie, remind yourself that you have been lying there for several minutes—as you have for many nights in the past—and nothing bad has happened. Congratulate yourself for staying there, take a few deep breaths, close your eyes, and start up another movie. Eventually sleep will come.

I'm scared. I think my parents are going to get a divorce. I love both of them very much, but I don't know how to handle this problem.

Caroline, Texas

When you're afraid of something that might happen but that you can't control, get the facts. Talk to your parents about your fears: "I'm worried because you two argue so much. Are you going to get a divorce?" You might find that your fears are unfounded.

If you learn they *are* getting divorced, it's OK to ask for reassurance. If you ask, "Are we going to be all right?" you'll give them a chance to remind you they will always love you. Tell them you need to know they will both stay in your life— and that you don't have to choose between them. It's OK for you to love them both.

Don't let fear stop you from trying something new. When you feel anxious about tryouts or any other new activity, ask yourself a simple question: "Then what would happen?" Here's how your mental conversation might go.

"I'm afraid of trying out for a solo. I might start singing and forget the words!"

"Then what would happen?"

"I guess I'd have to start over."

"Then what would happen?"

"Then either I'd do it better or I'd still stink."

"Then what would happen?"

"Well, I might get to sing the solo, or I'd end up just singing with the rest of the choir."

"Then what would happen?"

"I guess after a while I wouldn't be that upset, because either one would be OK."

Most likely you'll realize that you can get through the experience no matter what. Be realistic with your answers and you'll see that, slowly, your fear weakens with every "Then what?"

5. Starting middle school

4. Trying out for choir

3. Taking a big test

2. Speaking up in class

1. Saying hi to the new girl

Overcoming fear is like climbing the stairs. Each time you do something that makes you a little nervous, you take one step further from being afraid. You can conquer your fear. Don't give up!

I Feel Anxious

Sometimes you may worry that something bad **could happen** in the future. Sometimes you worry about something that's **not likely to happen** at all. Other times you feel uneasy for no particular reason. What's up?

I worry too much about whether my parents will be home when I get off the school bus. I have a list of phone numbers I can call if there's a problem, but I still worry. Can you help me?

Worrywart

Take things step by step. Make a list of situations you're afraid might happen, and with your parents' help, come up with a plan for how you'd handle each one. Then take a dry run. Ask your parents to be home but in the next room when you arrive, and walk through everything you'd do if they weren't there—make calls, ask for assistance, and so on. You'll feel calmer with them close by, and if you get stuck, they can help.

Next, practice coming home while your parents are waiting next door. If you take it one step at a time, you'll see you can handle all the scenarios on your list.

I worry about everything—tornadoes, heart attacks, all types of health problems. My mom thinks it's crazy, but I can't help it.

Caitlin, North Carolina

Between the news and crime dramas on TV, you may hear about a whole lot of scary things that can happen to people. You may feel anxious that something similar will happen to you. Some people worry a lot about events that are not very likely to occur. But worry is a feeling, not a solution.

Do a little experiment: Plan a few hours of activities with friends. During that time, stay busy. Whenever you start to worry about bad things that could happen, think "Stop!" and put your focus back on your friends and activities. When the time is up and things are just fine, congratulate yourself for not tying yourself into a worry knot!

I feel a lot of anxiety about school. My parents expect a lot from me. When I got a bad grade in math, they were disappointed—and so was I. What can I do to not stress out so much about schoolwork?

Laura, Illinois

Your parents might be disappointed with grades that are not as good as they know you could get, but that doesn't mean they don't love you. Even when they seem frustrated, their love for you is so strong that it can't be shaken by something like a bad grade. They may be angry at the situation, but they care deeply about you—don't forget that.

But there are things you can do to reduce your anxiety. If you can't fall asleep at night because you're worried about the test on Friday, don't lie there tossing and turning. Ask yourself this question: *Is there anything I can do right now to solve this problem?* Then think it through.

Is there anything I can do right now to solve this problem?

Yes. I can get up and figure out how much time I have to study and how many chapters I need to review.

No way. It's 11 p.m.! I need to sleep.

You've looked at your schedule and made your list. Is there anything else you can do now?

I'll come up with a plan first thing tomorrow.

Yes. I could start studying right now! But it's so late that I'll be exhausted tomorrow if I do.

No. It's too late.

Let it go. You've done all you can do for now.

Let it go. You have a plan and you've done all you can do for now.

I'm So Jealous

They don't call jealousy **the green-eyed monster** for nothing. When other people get more attention than you do, it can feel as if a beast has taken hold of you and turned you into someone you don't even know!

My friend is a really good gymnast. She can do three kinds of splits and all sorts of cool stuff. I thought I was good until I saw her. What should I do about the way I feel?

Charisse, New York

If you think about it, you wouldn't want your friend to do less than her very best. When she does a great stunt on the beam or an impressive tumbling run, try to congratulate her with a smile that's genuine.

If you can't shake your feelings of jealousy, you might need to have a serious talk with yourself. You are a worthwhile person even if you don't measure up to your friend's accomplishments. Remind yourself that you don't have to be perfect to enjoy your sport. You can also set a goal for improving your own skills—but work toward that goal for yourself, not to get the approval of others. Keep practicing, and be sure to pat yourself on the back for working so hard.

You did the right thing by trying to communicate with your cousin about the situation. Now the ball is in his court. If he doesn't get back to you, this may be one situation you just have to accept as gracefully as you can.

That doesn't have to stop you from having a good time at the wedding, though. Get involved in the festivities rather than slinking away feeling angry and hurt. Ask if there are ways you can be helpful, such as by managing the guest book or handing out rice. Or dance your heart out at the reception. Tell yourself that your day will come—and be happy for your sister.

I've Been Disrespected

Being picked on, teased, or bullied can really hurt. But you can learn how to respond and **keep your self-respect.**

The girls in my class are mean and play tricks on me. They think it's funny to hurt my feelings. What should I do? This has been happening to me for years, and I am getting sick of it!

Fed Up and Hurt

Being picked on can really hurt. To stand up for yourself, you need to state the problem, say you want it to stop, and do so in a way that lets you be on good terms with that person.

It'll take some guts. When someone teases you, take a deep breath and state exactly what you don't like. Practice your words beforehand. They can be as simple as, "It really hurts my feelings when you play tricks on me." Tell her what you want: "I want you to stop."

Talk to the bully in a way that can help you be on good terms. You might try, "It's not OK with me when you say mean things. I'd like to find a way for us to get along."

If the bully doesn't stop, you will at least have shown her— and those around her—that you are calm, you know what you want, and you're not afraid to stand up for yourself.

> People make fun of me because I'm overweight and have pimples. I do well in school, which others think is not cool. They call me "Brains" and "Four Eyes." Last year I cried every day about it, and sometimes I still cry.
>
> *Becca, California*

People who tease others in a mean-spirited way usually are immature and trying to feel better about themselves. Other kids may join in out of fear that if they don't, they will get picked on, too.

Even in the meanest of groups, though, there usually are a few people who don't get as involved in the tormenting. Focus on one of these girls as someone you could become better friends with. Try to get to know her better. Ask your parents if you can have her over sometime. Meet with your teacher privately and see if she can make some new rules about classroom behavior—ones that reward people who are kind to others.

Some kids make fun of my clothes and say I wear unpopular brands. It really hurts me, and sometimes I cry. I don't talk to my parents about it, because my mom has her own ideas about what I should wear. What can I do to feel better?

Dressed to Distress

Sometimes the best thing you can do is not let on that your feelings are hurt. If you like the clothes you wear, act calm so that it doesn't show you're bothered.

If you'd like to change your style, try to get your mother to remember what she was like at your age. Ask her if she ever felt out of step when she was young, and see if you can compromise on a few items of clothing that would help you stand out a little less.

Remember that no matter what you wear, if you wear it as though you love it—with your head high and a smile on your face—you will look a hundred times better than you would with a scowl. If you act comfortable with yourself, others may even respect you for your courage to be different.

I'm Angry

Everyone gets mad. What's important is staying in charge of how you let your angry feelings out.

I get mad a lot at little things that happen. I try to tell my family about them, but they either don't listen or telling them makes it worse. Most of the time I don't show that I'm upset, but I go to my room and cry. I don't know what to do.

Abby, North Carolina

It's frustrating when people don't seem to understand how you feel. You're taking a good first step by trying to talk with your family. Next, take a look at how you tell other people you are angry.

If you start out blaming the other person—such as, by telling your brother, "You always leave me out"—he is likely to defend himself with, "No way! I don't do that!" He might even blame you back. Try using "I statements" about how you feel ("I feel left out when you don't ask my opinion."). If you explain how you feel instead of pointing fingers, the other person is more likely to hear what you say—and that will make it easier to work out a solution.

When someone does something bad to me, all these angry emotions come pouring out and I act mean. I don't know how to stop myself.

Bonnie, Pennsylvania

If you're the kind of girl who explodes when she's angry, learn to recognize the signs that you're reaching your boiling point. Does your face get hot? Do your palms sweat? Do you start breathing fast? As soon as you feel these reactions coming on, tell yourself to stop and walk away. It's OK to say to the other person that you have to think for a minute about what just happened.

Or take a few deep breaths and count to ten. Head for your room, where you can punch or scream into a pillow. All of these tactics will help you get things under control. Then you can go back to the situation ready to discuss your feelings or move on with what needs to happen next.

In softball I get really mad if I don't play well. If I strike out, I find myself crying. I'm afraid everyone thinks I'm a bad sport. What can I do?

Maura, Alabama

Every athlete makes mistakes now and then. It's part of playing any sport. But how you react when you're down can determine whether you are a winner or a whiner. You're putting a lot of pressure on yourself to do well, and you're keeping track of everything you do wrong. Stop looking for your mistakes. Instead, at the end of the game, congratulate yourself on five things you did well ("I played hard," "I was a good sport," "I caught that fly ball," and so on). When you think about an error you made on a play, focus on what you can do to correct it next time. Visualize yourself executing the play correctly.

When you are trying as hard as you can, it's easy to forget that even the most competitive teams are playing a game that is supposed to be fun. If you aren't having fun, consider doing something else with your time.

If You Lose Your Cool

Do you need to smooth things over with someone after a blowup?
Try words like these once you have both cooled off.

I didn't like fighting with you.

I know I didn't act the best I could have.

I'm sorry that I _____ (yelled, slammed the door, called you that name).

Next time, I'll try to tell you what is bothering me before I get to that point.

It might help me stay calm if you would _____ (not point your finger, stop and listen to what I'm saying, ask how I'm feeling).

I'm Lonely

Loneliness can strike when you miss someone or when it seems as if everyone else is having more fun than you are. It can even happen when you're in a room full of people.

My parents are divorced, and I go to my dad's house every other weekend. When I am with him, I am lonely for my mom. When I'm with my mom, I'm lonely for my dad. How can I not miss them so much?

Missing Mom or Dad

It's hard being away from your mom or dad. But when you're at one parent's house, you don't have to forget about the other parent. Take a picture of your mom with you to your dad's, and arrange to call her at an agreed-upon time. The same goes for when you're visiting your mother.

Are there other emotions going on, too? Are you worried about the parent who's home without you or wondering if he or she might be worried about you? Are you concerned that your other parent's feelings might be hurt if you have too much fun? The best thing you can do is talk with your parents about your feelings and ask them to help reassure you. Then focus on enjoying the parent you are with right at that moment.

Sometimes I feel invisible. Every day on the bus my best friend sits and talks to me—until her friend Ashley gets on. Then she turns around and completely ignores me. It makes me very mad and I show it. It hurts a lot, and sometimes I want to cry.

The Invisible Girl

Quiet people often get left out of busy discussions, but that doesn't mean their friends like them any less. It's possible your friend isn't aware of what she's doing. She may even think she's dividing her time equally between you and Ashley. Talk to her alone and tell her how you feel.

Remember that your behavior can affect the way others respond to you. If you turn pouty and rude when Ashley gets on the bus, your actions tell your friends you don't want to be around them and make them less likely to want to spend time with you. Don't forget that you can talk with other kids on the bus, too. Your friend doesn't have to be your only bus buddy.

When my friends and I go bowling or do other group activities, I am always the one who is left out or who isn't talking with the group. I feel lonely, as if I don't fit in.

All by Myself

There are things you can do to get along better in a crowd. You don't have to be the life of the party, but when you feel lonely, reach out to the people around you! Find someone who isn't the center of attention to talk to. Ask her to show you how to figure the score. Ask her a question about herself. Tell her something that happened at school that day. Take orders for drinks!

Some people are just more comfortable doing things with only a few people instead of a large group. The next time you are heading for the bowling alley, plan ahead of time what you can do when you feel left out. Bring along a few snacks to share or memorize a joke to tell. You could also suggest a quieter activity that would draw the group together, such as playing a game or going out for ice cream.

I'm Really Sad

Just as you can bruise your leg or break your arm, sometimes it can feel as if your **whole heart hurts.** And when hopeless feelings stick around longer than usual, you need to get help.

I'm going through a lot of changes in my life, and I'm having a hard time handling all my feelings. I cry every night and I'm grumpy in the morning. I'm falling behind in my schoolwork. I don't know how to help myself.

Shea, Florida

When you feel sad, everything in life can seem more difficult. When sadness goes too far, your mood can definitely interfere with schoolwork and relationships. That, of course, just makes you feel worse! Getting active and fighting your blue mood may be the last thing you want to do. But gather up your strength and give these ideas a try:

Get your body moving! Climb the stairs, walk the dog, or mow the lawn. Get your heart pumping!

Get outdoors for a little while, even if it's cloudy or rainy. Breathe in some of that fresh air.

Let there be light! Open the curtains and turn on some lamps. Let the light shine in.

Eat healthy food. Even if you're not hungry, try to eat three meals (or five smaller meals) a day. Stay away caffeine, such as in chocolate and certain soft drinks. Caffeine can make it hard to sleep at night, and that's the last thing you need right now.

Don't let yourself sleep in on weekends. Go to bed and get up at your usual time.

Avoid negative people. Don't spend more time than you have to with people who make you feel bad.

Don't hide, either! Make yourself say hi to others, invite someone over, or ask a friend to go to a movie.

Ask your parents to help if you are feeling overwhelmed by your chores, activities, or homework.

Draw a picture or make a sculpture of your feelings—art can help to get emotions out in front of you.

Express your sadness or anger by **writing.**

> Sometimes I worry because I cry a lot. If one of my friends says something mean or if I don't get a good grade, I feel so sad. Then everything around me seems gloomy.
>
> ## Down in the Dumps

When things don't go the way you wish they would, everything around you can start to look glum. It's natural that your friends are going to disappoint you once in a while and that sometimes you might disappoint yourself. It's also normal to feel sad when those things happen.

Let the sadness wash over you. Cry if you need to. Then pick yourself up and try to put whatever upset you in perspective. Make a mental list of your good qualities—you know you have them. Think about whether your not-so-great grade really means the end of the world. Then move on. In time your sadness may just go away on its own.

I've started to notice my feelings hurt a lot more. My grandmother has cancer, and I don't want to lose her. When my parents broke up, I cried myself to sleep. My grades are going down. I feel alone. I lock myself in my room and cry for hours. I need help.

Kayla, Texas

For some people, sadness gets severe and they can't shake the feeling that things are hopeless. These people may have depression. But don't get the idea that depressed people are weak or lazy. They have a serious illness, and they can get help from therapists who talk with them about their emotions and doctors who prescribe medication.

Signs of Depression

If you experience any of the feelings below, show this page to your parents and talk to them about whether a professional could help you. It doesn't always mean you have depression, but your sadness may be serious. Do you

- have sadness that lasts for more than two weeks?

- feel tired all the time?

- have difficulty paying attention or concentrating?

- often feel angry or irritable?

- not feel like doing things you usually enjoy?

- have frequent stomachaches or headaches?

- have bad feelings about yourself?

- think a lot about death or suicide?*

- feel that you could hurt yourself or someone else?*

*Note: No matter what you said to the rest of these items, if you said "yes" to either of the last two, tell an adult right away, and ask to talk to a psychologist or medical doctor.

I'm Grieving

It may happen when someone dies or when a friend moves away: you feel sad, angry, fearful, lonely, or a mix of painful emotions. The good news? You can **let yourself be sad, learn from it, and get through it.**

My grandfather just died, and I'm very sad. Nothing will ever be normal again. When I go to my grandma's house for the holidays, Grandpa won't be sitting in the big chair at the end of the table, making everybody laugh.

Corey, Illinois

Feeling grief can make you wonder how life will ever be fun again. No matter how much you hurt, the best thing you can do is to keep sharing with your family and friends. You need to release those sad feelings in order to move ahead with your life.

Talk to someone else who is missing your grandfather. Remember the good times you both had with him.

Honor the person who died. Don't ignore that your grandpa is gone. Start a new tradition, such as lighting a special candle for him at the holiday dinner.

Write a letter stating all the reasons you think he was wonderful. Share it with your grandma, turn it in as an essay at school, or keep it to read again later.

Make a photo album to remember the good times you had together. Or frame something special that belonged to him.

Distract yourself with things that take your mind off your sadness for a while. Go to a movie, play with friends, and even laugh. No doubt the person you are missing would want it that way.

What Happens?

There's no "right" way to grieve. You might act quiet and withdrawn, feel tense and irritable, or cry harder than you ever knew you could. You may go through all of these feelings in one week, in one day, or in one hour!

Most people go through a few typical stages when they are grieving, although they don't always experience them in the same order. At first they can't believe the loss is happening. They may ignore what is going on. Then they may get angry or scared about it, followed by feeling sad and hopeless. Finally, they learn to accept their loss and go on with their lives.

> When my grandmother died, I felt really bad that I was too busy playing to even talk to her the last time I saw her.
> *Guilty Conscience*

It is easy to feel guilty about things you did or didn't do with a loved one who has died. Maybe you didn't say "I love you" the last time you talked. Maybe you were irritated or distracted.

It's OK to have regrets about how you acted, but every time you let guilt into your head and your heart, it chips away at you. You can't rewrite the past. Admit you made a mistake, but then try to let it go. If you want, apologize to the person who died—in your journal, in a letter you write to her, or in your thoughts. Think about times you felt close to your grandma and the good times you shared. Remember that people have a way of knowing how you really feel about them. No doubt your grandmother did, too.

My best friend is moving away! I've known her since preschool, and I'm so afraid to lose her. I don't know what to do.

Friendless Forever?

When a friend moves, it can feel almost as sad as a death. It's hard to imagine every day without your dearest friend—and you don't want to. Worst of all, there's nothing you can do to stop it from happening. The good thing is you can stay friends, if you're willing to work at it. Your friend will still be out there for you to talk, e-mail, and write to. She'll just be farther away.

Before she leaves, have an envelope party to make it easier to keep in touch: Put your address and a postage stamp on a stack of envelopes, and have her do the same. Exchange stacks with a promise to stick notes and pictures in the envelopes every now and then and drop them in the mail.

After she's gone, make an effort to get together with kids you don't know as well. Your best friend will always have a special place in your heart, but there's room in there for new friends, too.

I Don't Feel Safe

Watching the bad things that show up on the news and in movies leaves many girls feeling scared, even in places where they should feel safe. **How do you handle it when you're worried about something happening in your life?**

My dad is in the military and is going overseas for a little over a year. I'm really scared that something bad will happen to him while he's away. But I'm also worried about my mom and me being safe on our own at home.

Fearing for My Family

When something scary happens in the world, you may wonder what it would be like if it happened to you or to someone you love. Try not to spend too much time watching the news or imagining bad things happening. Instead, do some positive things, such as finding out how you can send letters or e-mails to your dad, or thinking about what you and your friends could make or collect to send to him when he is overseas to help with what he is doing.

Tell your mom if you are concerned about the two of you staying home. She can explain what she will be doing to take care of things while your dad is away. Make plans to spend extra time with your friends and other family members. And remind yourself that many, many people—from the president to the military to police officers—are doing things around the world to make sure you and the people you love stay secure.

I worry about school shootings. Once a boy brought a gun to my school. He was caught before anybody was hurt, but it was scary. I still don't know why it happened.

A Scared Student

This must have been a very scary experience—one you can be sure no one wants to happen again. Knowing more about why it happened can put your mind at rest. Ask your teacher or school counselor if she can explain what went on and why the boy brought the gun. How did the teachers stop him, and what is being done now to keep people safe?

Find out who to tell if you notice anything that concerns you in the future. Talk to your parents, too. They will want to be sure you feel safe. Ask them for reassurance that they think your school is a safe place to be.

My house caught on fire last month, and I thought I was going to die. Smoke was everywhere and I was terrified. The fire trucks came and put out the fire, but everything of ours burned, even my stuffed animals. My friends have been really understanding, and we are moving to a new house soon, but I'm really afraid of that house burning down, too.

Melissa, Nebraska

You've lost a lot, and it's normal for you to be sad and a little fearful. Fortunately, you're safe and you can begin to build your life again. Although moving might make you nervous, the chances of a house fire ever happening to you again are very, very small. You can help yourself relax by making a clear safety plan wherever you live: know that there are fire alarms, what your escape route would be, and how you'd call for help.

Other kids can learn from your experience. You and your family are now experts on how to survive a house fire. Ask your teacher if you can talk with your class about making their own safety plans. People who have been through traumatic experiences often feel better when they educate others.

Your memories of the fire and what you've lost will be strong and painful, especially now. But if you stay active, keep talking to friends and family, and focus on the good things ahead of you, each day will get a little easier.

Getting Back to Normal

Right after a disaster happens, people may feel shock, fear, anger, sadness, or guilt. This is a time to be especially kind to yourself and those around you. Take care of your body and your mind, and take time to sort out your emotions. In addition to talking about your feelings, eating right, and getting enough sleep, you should try these things:

Keep a routine. Continue as many of your everyday activities as possible. Following a routine makes your world more predictable.

Remember soccer practice at 3:00!

Turn off the TV. Watch just enough to be informed, but don't keep going over the trauma. And stay away from scary movies, too.

Talk to others who went through the disaster. Pull your family closer by talking to them and doing activities together.

Keep with a good crowd. Hang around people who are calm and don't listen to those who spread rumors.

Distract yourself a little! It's still OK to do things you enjoy and have fun with your friends.

Feeling Positive

Most of the time in your life, you'll feel pretty good about other people, the future, and yourself. But when you don't, **you'll have the skills you need** to get through the hard times—and help others get through them, too.

The Good Stuff

You've read a lot about difficult feelings such as anger, sadness, and fear. But feelings can be positive, too. Enjoy those good feelings and remember them during the rough times. (Circle) the positive emotions you felt last week.

I felt...

glad

hopeful

safe

optimistic

trustful

competent

able

inspired

strong

capable

proud

joyful

awed

excited

confident

grateful

happy

silly

Look Around!

Knowing how emotions work can help you understand other people and be considerate of their feelings. **How could you be most helpful** when your friends show their emotions? Circle the best answer.

1. Your good friend Noah blows up at you for losing his book. In a fit of anger, he calls you stupid and says you always mess things up. You

    a. tell him all the things he's done wrong in the past.
    b. apologize and tell him you'll buy him a new book. Mention later that you didn't think it was appropriate for him to call you a name.
    c. walk away and forget it. Who needs him for a friend, anyway?

2. Your best friend, Sophie, wins a math contest and is dancing around in the gym as if she just scored a touchdown. Other people are rolling their eyes. You

    a. decide that Sophie is terribly conceited and that you don't like her anymore.
    b. march out of the gym in a huff. Doesn't she care that you didn't even get third place?
    c. congratulate Sophie and whisper to her that she might want to calm down just a bit.

3. Trent's dog died over the weekend, but the kids at school are too busy to notice that he is sitting alone on the playground and has tears in his eyes. You

   a. yell at the other kids for not being sensitive.
   b. stay away from him because other people's sadness makes you sad, too.
   c. tell him you are sorry about his dog and let him know you care how he feels.

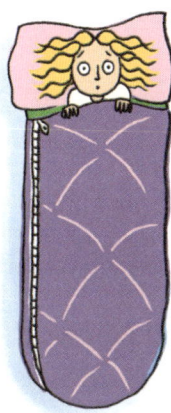

4. At your slumber party, you and Lauren are the only ones still awake. She confides that she's afraid and can't go to sleep. You

   a. offer to leave the light on in the hall and tell her how you visualize a peaceful scene to relax.
   b. tell her to be quiet—hey, you're trying to catch some ZZZs.
   c. wake the others and tell them Lauren's being a baby.

Answers:

If you gave the following answers, you understand that emotions can be strong and that people don't always react to them in the most positive ways. Your sensitivity makes you a great friend!

1. b. You know that Noah is just blowing off steam. You are right to offer to fix your mistake and to wait until he has cooled off to request he behave differently next time.

2. c. Sophie might not realize she is being annoying, but telling her that in an obvious way would only embarrass her and make her angry with you. Good for you for being sensitive and happy for her.

3. c. Trent is likely to appreciate your sympathy. You might even create a friendship that wasn't there before.

4. a. There's a good chance Lauren will relax once she knows she is not alone with her fear. Being sensitive to your friend's anxiety is the kind thing to do.

Keep It Up!

So, the big question: **Is it OK to feel this way?** You bet. Every experience you have, and the way you feel about it, can teach you something about yourself and help you grow. But remember, with every angry word (and with every smile) you are painting a picture of yourself in your mind—and for others to see. Be sure it's a painting you like. If you don't, now is the time to do something about it.

Take time to listen to your feelings and share them with others the best way you know how. Use the skills you learned in this book to help figure them out. If you want to learn even more, *The Feelings Book Journal* can help you sort out specific emotions and suggest things you can do about them. The better you become at understanding and expressing your feelings, the more you will enjoy being you!

The Care & Keeping of
YOU
Journal
1
for Younger Girls

Cara Natterson, MD, Medical Consultant
illustrated by Josée Masse

Published by American Girl Publishing
Copyright © 2001, 2008, revised ed. © 2013 by American Girl

Questions or comments? Call 1-800-845-0005, visit **americangirl.com**,
or write to Customer Service, American Girl, 8400 Fairway Place,
Middleton, WI 53562-0497.

Printed in China
13 14 15 16 17 18 19 LEO 10 9 8 7 6 5 4 3 2 1

Editorial Development: Elizabeth A. Chobanian, Michelle Watkins,
Therese Kauchak Maring, Carrie Anton, Barbara Stretchberry

Art Direction & Design: Chris Lorette David, Camela Decaire

Production: Janette Sowinski, Lori Armstrong, Lisa Bunescu,
Jeannette Bailey, Kristi Tabrizi, Judith Lary, Tami Kepler

Illustrations: Josée Masse

Medical Consultants: Dr. Lia Gaggino, Pediatrician; Dr. Cara
Natterson, MD

This book is not intended to replace the advice of or treatment by
physicians, psychologists, or other health-care professionals. It
should be considered an additional resource only. Questions and
concerns about mental or physical health should always be discussed
with a doctor or other health-care provider.

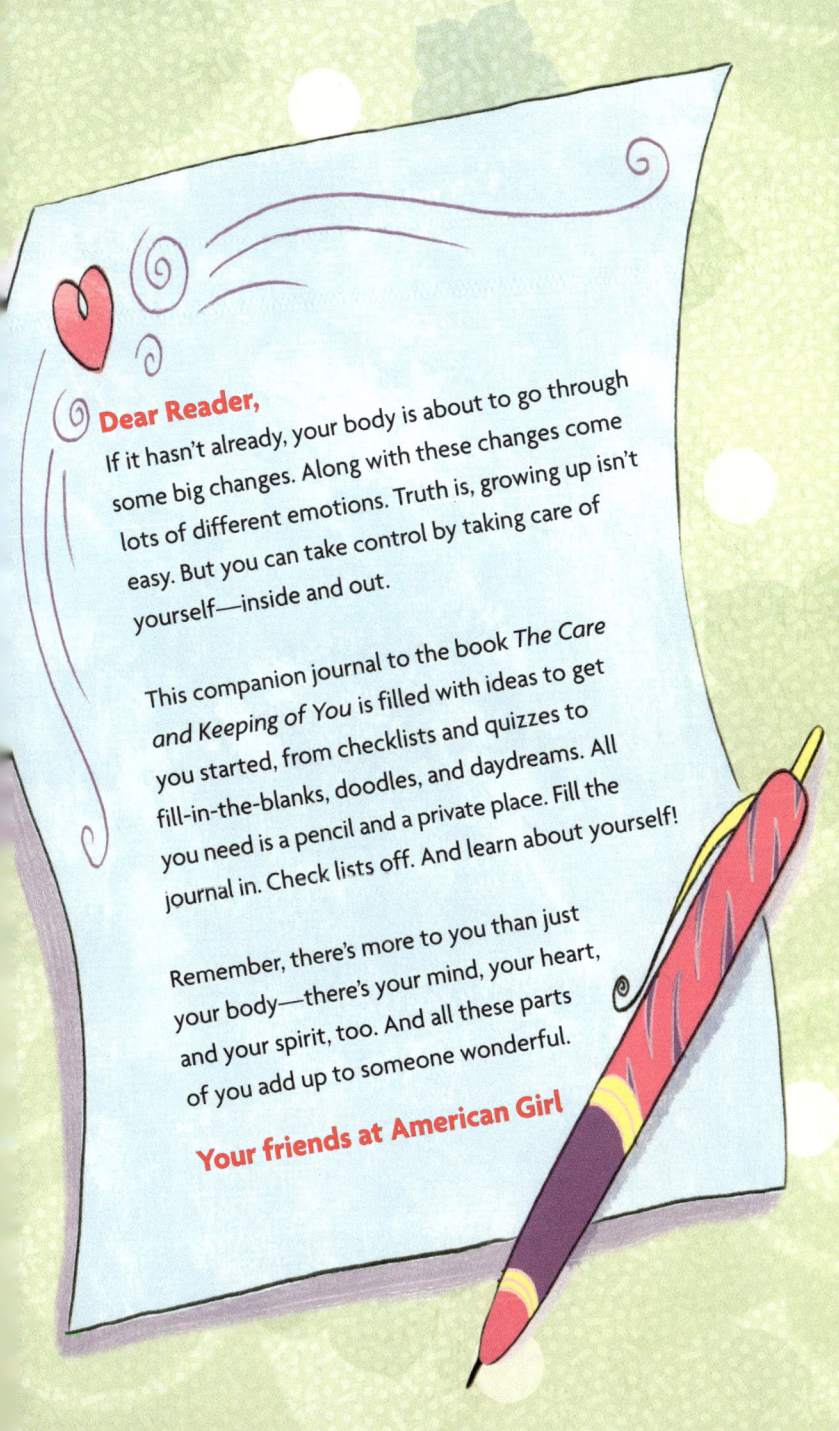

Dear Reader,

If it hasn't already, your body is about to go through some big changes. Along with these changes come lots of different emotions. Truth is, growing up isn't easy. But you can take control by taking care of yourself—inside and out.

This companion journal to the book *The Care and Keeping of You* is filled with ideas to get you started, from checklists and quizzes to fill-in-the-blanks, doodles, and daydreams. All you need is a pencil and a private place. Fill the journal in. Check lists off. And learn about yourself!

Remember, there's more to you than just your body—there's your mind, your heart, and your spirit, too. And all these parts of you add up to someone wonderful.

Your friends at American Girl

About Me

You are more than just the reflection you see in the mirror. Your mind, body, and spirit make you unique.

Mind

My favorite subject in school is ....

I'm fascinated by ....

....

I want to learn more about ....

....

I love to read ....

....

I love to write ....

....

Body

Age: ....

Height: ....

I'm ☐ left-handed ☐ right-handed

Spirit

Time of day I'm at my best: ....

People I love: ....

....

Things that make me happy: ....

Things that make me sad: ....

Best friends: ....

....

Things I wish I could change about the world: ....

....

....

Who Am I Like?

No one will ever be exactly like you. But chances are you see similarities between yourself and your parents or relatives. How are you like another member of your family?

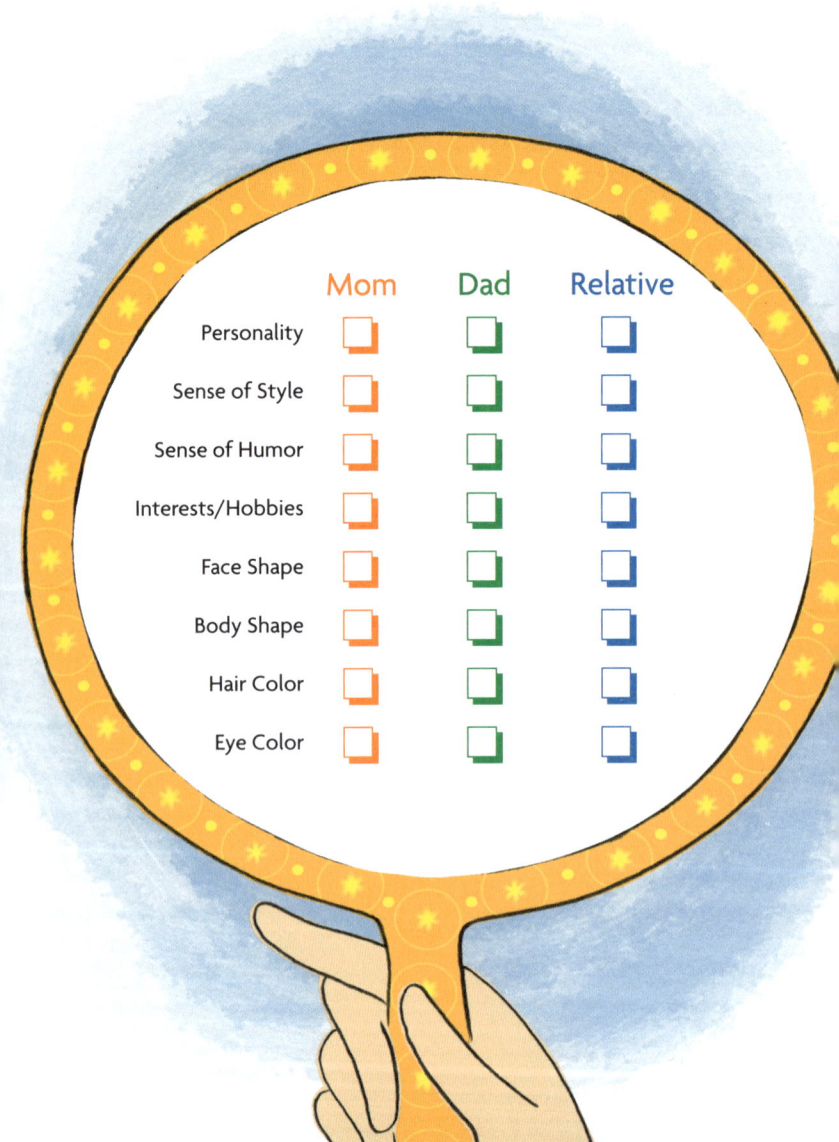

	Mom	Dad	Relative
Personality	☐	☐	☐
Sense of Style	☐	☐	☐
Sense of Humor	☐	☐	☐
Interests/Hobbies	☐	☐	☐
Face Shape	☐	☐	☐
Body Shape	☐	☐	☐
Hair Color	☐	☐	☐
Eye Color	☐	☐	☐

Inside and out, here's what makes me uniquely me:

I Am . . .

Circle the words that best describe you.

Caring

Thoughtful

Giggly

Funny

Clever

Serious

Outrageous

Kind

Dedicated

Musical

Honest Happy Quiet

Clumsy Artistic Smart

Athletic

Talkative

Goofy

Loyal

Sensitive

Hard-working

Informed

Creative

Colorful Assertive

Sincere

Affectionate

Warm

Lazy

physical

Shy

Compassionate

Silly

Studious

Courteous

Fearful

polite

Friendly

Energetic

Bold

Moody

Independent

Logical

Messy

Loving

Easy-going

Irritable

Loud

Stylish

Proud

Gentle

Top three words I would use
to describe myself:

Carefree

1. ....

2. ....

Theatrical

3. ....

Here's Why!

How do the words you chose on the previous page match how you think, act, or feel?

Word **1.** _____ describes me because

_____

_____

_____

_____

_____

_____

_____

_____

_____

_____

Word **2.** .... describes me because ....

....

....

....

....

....

Word **3.** .... describes me because ....

....

....

....

....

....

Style File

Everyone has her own special style. What's yours?
Fill these pages with clippings, photos, and doodles
of things that say **you.**

Making the Grade

As you get older, the list of things you can do gets longer. Think of this as your own personal report card—a tally of all the things you're good at, as well as the skills you'd like to improve.

	I'm awesome at	I'm good at	I'm OK at	I wish I were better at
Math	☐	☐	☐	☐
English	☐	☐	☐	☐
Science	☐	☐	☐	☐
Social Studies	☐	☐	☐	☐
Music	☐	☐	☐	☐
Art	☐	☐	☐	☐
Sports	☐	☐	☐	☐

	I'm awesome at	I'm good at	I'm OK at	I wish I were better at
Listening	☐	☐	☐	☐
Sharing	☐	☐	☐	☐
Positive Thinking	☐	☐	☐	☐
Organizing	☐	☐	☐	☐
Communicating	☐	☐	☐	☐

Three other things I'm awesome at:

1. ....

2. ....

3. ....

Goal-Getter

Take one thing you wish you were better at and set a specific goal.

I wish I were better at ....

....

My specific goal is to ....

....

Who can help me and how they can help: ....

....

....

....

....

....

....

....

....

Three things I'll do to achieve my goal:

1.

2.

3.

Roadblocks and how I'll get past them:

How long and how often I'll work on my goal:

Changes

You're going through some pretty big changes—inside and out. Compare how you were a year ago to how you are today. Write about the changes that have taken place:

At school:

At home:

To my body:

In my friendships:

In my interests:

How these changes make me feel:

Changes I'm waiting for:

Taking Care of Myself

Take control of your growing body by taking care of it. Now it's more important than ever, while you're going through big changes. It may feel as if there's a lot to remember, but the following lists will help you break things down. Check off the ones you already do.

Every Day

☐ Wash my face (morning and night) with mild soap or cleanser and warm water

☐ Brush my teeth and tongue and floss my teeth (in the morning and at night, and when possible after eating)

☐ Shower or bathe with soap

☐ Apply deodorant as needed

☐ Clean my newly pierced earlobes (three times a day with a cleanser recommended by the technician)

☐ Wash my hands with soap after I use the bathroom and before I eat

☐ Comb or brush my hair

☐ Get at least ten hours of sleep

☐ Clean my contacts or eyeglasses

☐ Drink enough water to stay hydrated

☐ Exercise enough to get sweaty (60 minutes a day)

At Least Weekly

❑ Wash my hair regularly (as needed)

❑ Wash my hairbrushes and combs

❑ Trim my nails

Once or Twice a Year

❑ See the doctor for a physical exam (once a year)

❑ See the dentist for a dental exam (twice a year)

❑ See the eye doctor for an eye exam
(as needed)

Here are some other things I do to take care of myself:

....

....

....

....

....

....

....

....

....

....

....

....

Bubble Trouble

Is bathing a bore?
Do you cower when
it's time to shower?
Are your mornings
filled with madness?
Follow the bubble
trail for tub tips!

Start here

Are you always rushing to get ready for school in the morning?

No

Yes

Shampoo, rinse, condition, rinse—does it take too long to wash your hair?

Are you bored with the same old showering routine?

Does having wet hair give you the willies?

Does your hair get really tangled after you wash it?

Are you ready to jump out as soon as you jump in?

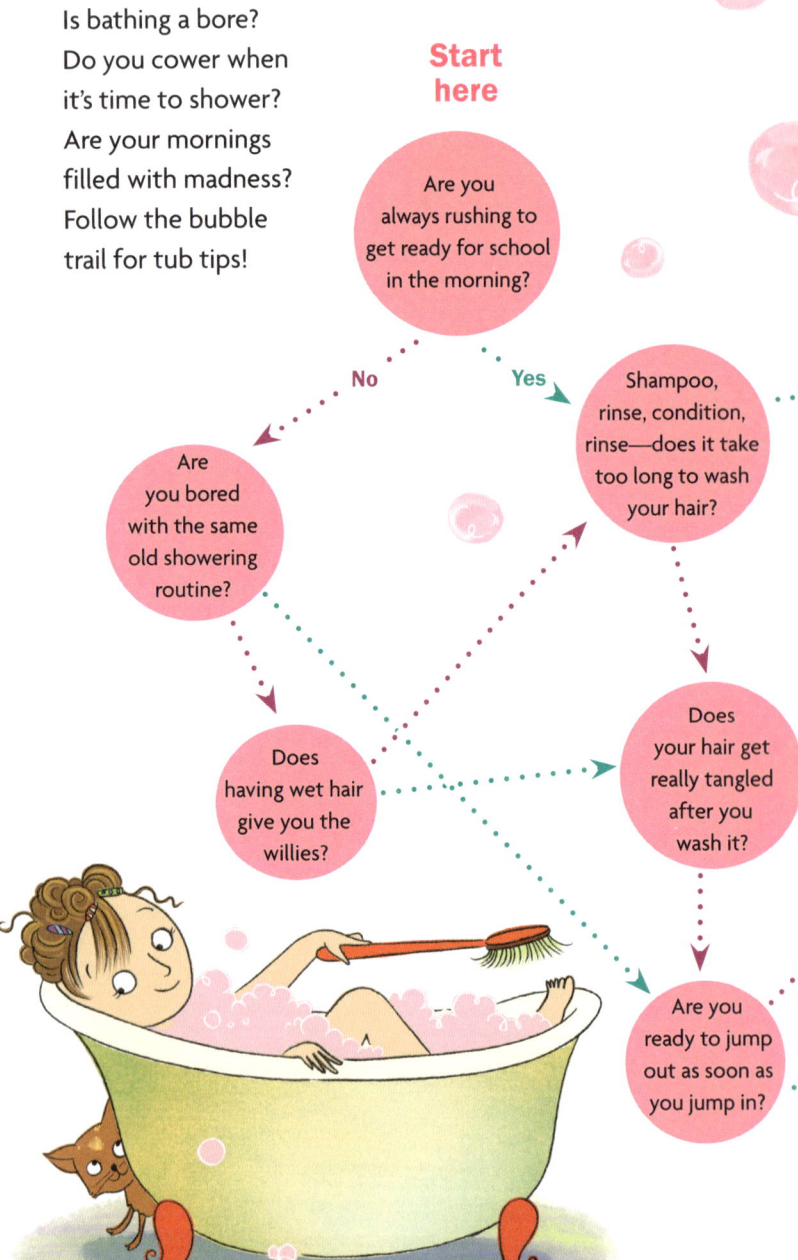

Do you wish there was a speedier way to get clean?

Timely Tips

You need to save time in the shower. Try showering at night instead of in the morning, and you won't feel so rushed before school. Use a shampoo/ conditioner combo to save time. And don't use too much. A small squirt is all you need, and it will rinse out faster than a handful.

Is taking care of your hair a hassle?

Hair Scare

All tangled up? Here are a few tips for easier hair care. Don't rub your hair dry with a towel. Instead, pat it—it won't get as tangled. And keep in mind, the shorter your hair is, the less time it'll take to dry. No matter what length your hair is, make sure you get it trimmed regularly to help prevent tangles.

Do you just want showering to be more fun?

Shower Power

It might be time for a new showering routine. If you've been using the same bath products for a long time, try a new brand of soap or shampoo. A fresh scent will perk you up! Trade in your washcloth for a cute puff. And sing your favorite tunes while you shower— your voice will sound great!

Pampering Myself

Ten ways to boost your mind, body, and spirit:

Soak in a warm bubble bath.

Take a walk.

Dance—put on music that makes you feel happy, and let yourself go!

Relax. Stretch, close your eyes, breathe deeply—whatever makes you calm.

Lend a helping hand—being a friend to others will make you feel good, too.

Write it down—keep a journal of thoughts, feelings, and dreams.

Express yourself—talk to a friend, parent, or teacher.

Laugh—watch a favorite sitcom, cartoon, or movie.

Get moving—boost your spirits by getting your body in motion.

Treat your feet—pamper your toes with a scrub, lotion, and pretty nail polish.

Here's what makes me feel relaxed and pampered:

Feeling Good

Good health starts on the inside. Write about the things you do that make you feel happy and healthy.

Battling Bad Habits

If you bite your nails or pick at your face, you're not alone. The good news is that lots of girls have been able to break their bad habits once they put their minds to it. The key to reaching a goal is to write it down. The more specific you are about your plan, the more likely you are to succeed!

My bad habits:

Choose one bad habit from your list that you'd like to break.

Bad habit I'm going to break:

I'll completely break my bad habit by this date:

My daily plan of attack:

Here's how I'll reward myself:

Hair Hotline

The key to a great 'do is accepting how your hair is naturally. And remember, clean and healthy hair is the best look of all! Circle the qualities natural to your hair. Then underline qualities of your dream hair.

Blonde

Brunette

Brown

Black

Red

Curly

Smooth

Straight

Short

Thick

Long

Wavy

Soft

Thin

Oily

Shoulder-length

Bouncy

Auburn

Dry

I wish I had my dream hair because

....

....

....

....

Good things about my hair just the way it is:

....

....

....

....

....

....

....

Things I can do with my hair when I need a change:

☐ Clip it

☐ Put it in a ponytail or pigtails

☐ Braid it

☐ Tie it back with a scarf

Hair Doodles

A drawing of myself . . .

. . . on a **good hair day**

. . . on a **bad hair day**

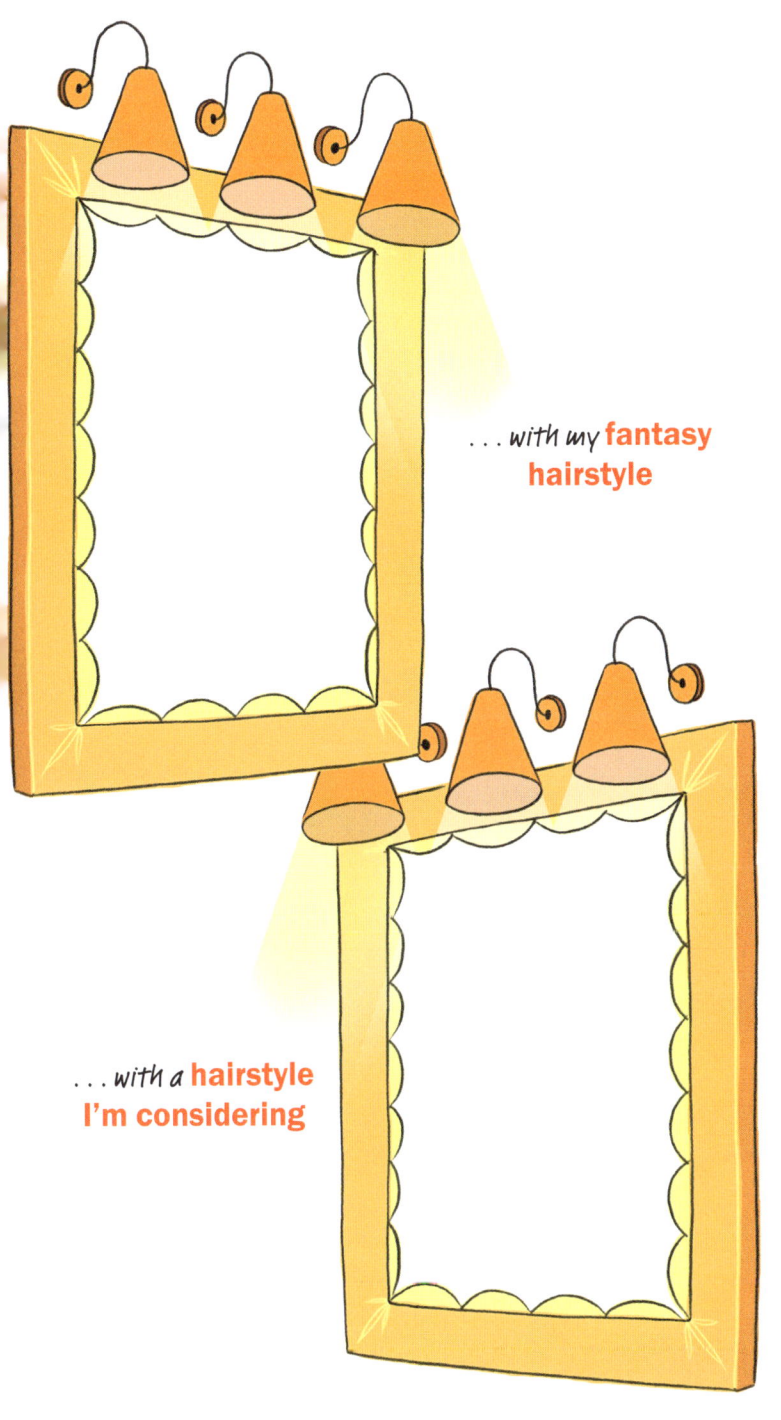

. . . with my **fantasy hairstyle**

. . . with a **hairstyle I'm considering**

Serve Yourself!

Just how much from each food group should you eat every day? That depends on your age and how physically active you are. The United States Department of Agriculture (USDA) says that a girl who is ten years old and gets 60 minutes of moderate to vigorous exercise a day should aim to eat this:

Fruits, such as
- bananas
- oranges
- raisins
- apples
- peaches
- pears

Grains, such as
- whole wheat
- popcorn
- oats
- brown rice
- wild rice

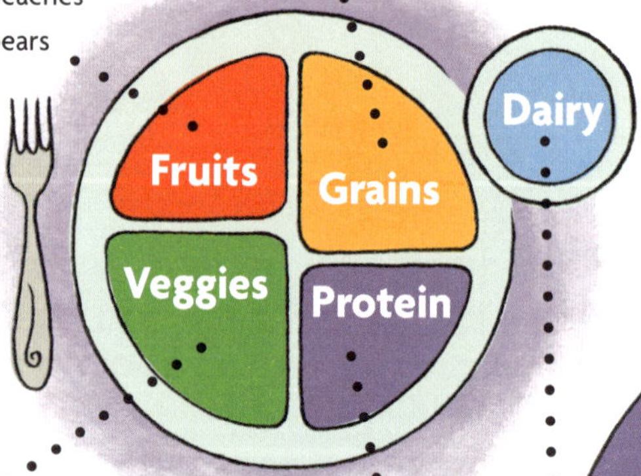

Fruits

Grains

Dairy

Veggies

Protein

Vegetables, such as
- spinach
- tomatoes
- avocado
- cucumbers
- green peas
- acorn squash

Proteins, such as
- chicken or turkey
- beef
- almonds, peanuts, and other nuts and nut butters
- salmon, tuna, and other fish
- tofu
- eggs

Dairy products, such as
- milk
- yogurt
- cheese
- calcium-fortified soy milk

Are you eating from each food group daily? Check off foods on the chart below for one day to see how you're doing.

	Breakfast	Lunch	Dinner	Snacks
Grains	☐	☐	☐	☐
Vegetables	☐	☐	☐	☐
Fruits	☐	☐	☐	☐
Dairy Products	☐	☐	☐	☐
Proteins	☐	☐	☐	☐

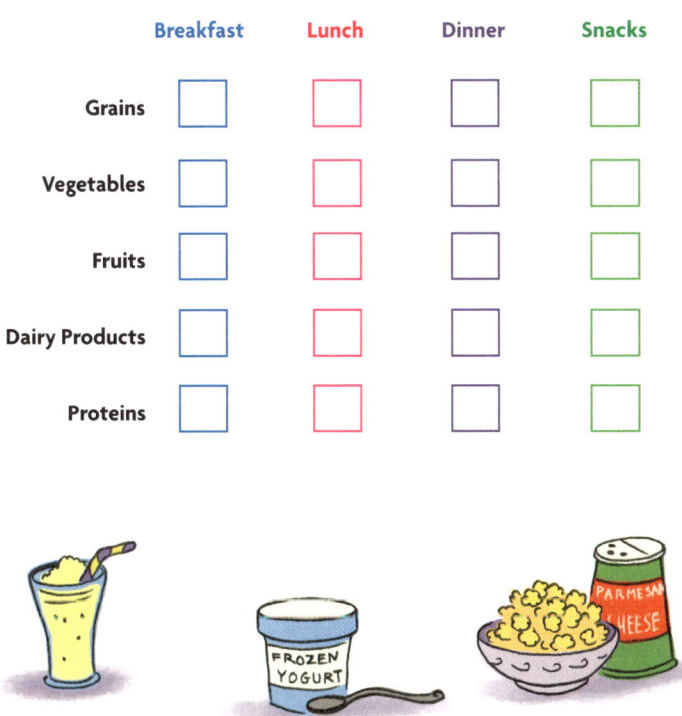

Don't forget water. Make sure you drink plenty of it every day, especially during and after exercise.

Healthy Choices

What I should be eating more of:

....

What I should be eating less of:

....

I ☐ am ☐ am not
drinking enough water.

Five healthy snacks I already
like to eat:

1. ....

2. ....

3. ....

4. ....

5. ....

If you were doing the grocery shopping for your family, what would be on your shopping list?

My Favorite Foods

What I eat for breakfast on school days: ....

....

What I eat for breakfast on weekends: ....

....

My favorite treat: ....

My favorite dinner: ....

When I'm sick, my favorite comfort foods are ....

....

I like to cook ....

....

....

I'd like to learn to cook ....

....

....

Here's a drawing of my favorite birthday cake:

My favorite memory of a dinner is ....

....

....

If I were a dessert, I would be ....

because ....

....

....

My Period

"Getting your period." There are probably few words that
will make you feel as excited, scared, or just plain confused.
Whether you've already started your period or you're still
waiting for it to start, being prepared will help you relax.

Keep these in
your backpack:

- One pad or
  tampon (A makeup
  bag or an eyeglass
  case is a good
  holder.)
- Spare pair of
  underwear

Keep these things at home:

- A box of pads or tampons
- A box of panty liners
- A calendar
- Medication for cramps
  (Talk to a parent about getting a
  pain reliever, if you need one, at
  the drugstore.)

It's natural to have lots of questions about your period. You'll feel more at ease once you get some answers. Start by pinpointing what's on your mind.

Check any questions that you're still wondering about:

- [ ] How will I know when my period is about to begin?

- [ ] How will it feel? Will it hurt?

- [ ] How long will it last?

- [ ] Will other people know when I have my period?

- [ ] How do I use a pad?

- [ ] How do I know what size pad to use?

- [ ] What should I do when I sleep at night?

- [ ] Can I exercise or swim when I have my period?

- [ ] When do I need to use a tampon?

Can We Talk?

When it comes to your period, the good news is that you're not alone. Every teenage girl or woman has had all the questions you have now. And no question is too silly or too embarrassing to ask. You may feel like crawling into a hole, but remember, getting your period is normal. Find your mom, aunt, or other adult you trust. Muster up your courage and ask, "Do you have time to talk?"

Three adults I feel comfortable talking to about my period and other tricky stuff:

1. ....

2. ....

3. ....

Steps that lead to a good conversation:

1. Pick a time when the other person isn't busy. Try bedtime, dinner, or when the two of you are doing something alone together.

2. Start with, "Can we talk?"

3. If you're embarrassed, admit it.

4. Say, "I've been thinking about _____, and I want to ask you a question."

5. Take a deep breath, and ask away.

Here are some questions I'd like to ask:

Writing a note to your mom or another trusted adult
might help if you're just too tongue-tied.

Keeping Track

At first, it can be tricky to predict when your periods will arrive. Use a calendar, such as the one to the right, to keep track of when they start and end. Put an X in the box for each day you have your period. Once your periods become regular, which usually happens within one to two years, they should last about the same length of time each month.

Don't be surprised if your periods are irregular, especially when you first start getting them.

	jan	feb	mar	apr	may	jun	jul	aug	sep	oct	nov	dec
1												
2												
3												
4												
5												
6												
7												
8												
9												
10												
11												
12												
13												
14												
15												
16												
17												
18												
19												
20												
21												
22												
23												
24												
25												
26												
27												
28												
29												
30												
31												

Period Patterns

Once you begin to menstruate regularly, you may notice patterns in how you feel physically and emotionally. If you're feeling achy or crabby, this is perfectly normal. By paying attention to how you feel, you can understand your cycle and be prepared.

My period lasts for about _____ days.

It's heaviest on day # _____ .

My Body

	Achy	Tired	So-So	Comfortable	Energized
Before	☐	☐	☐	☐	☐
During	☐	☐	☐	☐	☐
After	☐	☐	☐	☐	☐

My Mood

	Crabby	Sad	So-So	Happy	Psyched
Before	☐	☐	☐	☐	☐
During	☐	☐	☐	☐	☐
After	☐	☐	☐	☐	☐

Here's how I feel about my period:

Feeling Better

All of the following activities can make you feel better when you have your period. Check which ones work for you.

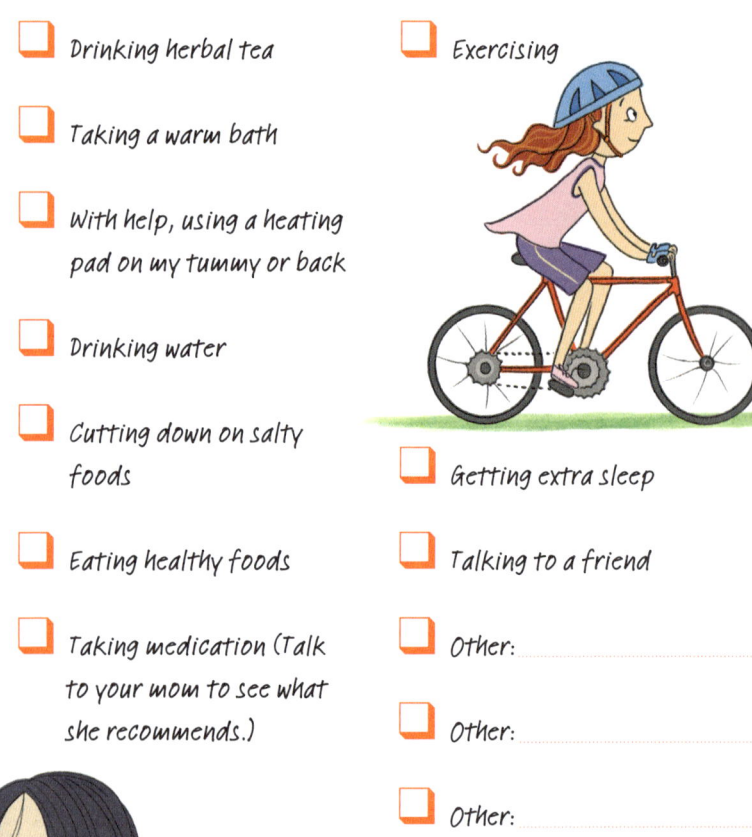

☐ Drinking herbal tea

☐ Taking a warm bath

☐ With help, using a heating pad on my tummy or back

☐ Drinking water

☐ Cutting down on salty foods

☐ Eating healthy foods

☐ Taking medication (Talk to your mom to see what she recommends.)

☐ Exercising

☐ Getting extra sleep

☐ Talking to a friend

☐ Other: ....

☐ Other: ....

☐ Other: ....

Writing down your thoughts can also make you feel better.
Use this page to "talk" about whatever's on your mind.

....

....

....

....

....

....

....

....

....

....

....

....

....

Feelings

Feel as if you're riding an emotional roller coaster? You're not going crazy—you're just growing up. The same hormones that tell your body to wake up and grow can strongly affect your feelings, too. Put an ✗ through all the feelings and your responses to them that get in the way of your good mood:

Loneliness

Exhaustion

Anger

Frustration

Embarrassment

Hopelessness

Jealousy

Rage

Selfishness

Stress

Depression

Uncertainty

Boredom

Restlessness

Sadness

Shame

Disappointment

Sulkiness

Meanness

Insecurity

Carelessness

Shyness

Nervousness

Irritability

Guilt

Competitiveness

Impatience

Confusion

Grouchiness

Fear

Disgust

Three things that make me crabby:

1. ....

....

2. ....

....

3. ....

....

Mood Makeovers

What do you do to change a bad mood into a good one?

 When I'm sad, I ....

....

....

 When I'm lonely, I ....

....

....

 When someone has hurt my feelings, I ....

....

....

When I'm frustrated, I ....

....

....

....

....

....

When I'm scared, I ....

....

....

....

....

If you feel stuck in a bad mood, let a grown-up
know. It is never silly to ask for help.

How I'm Feeling

Time out! How do you feel about all these changes? What are you thinking about your body right now? Use this space to pour out what's on your mind:

....

....

....

....

....

....

....

....

....

....

....

Heart-to-Heart

Start a conversation with a woman you know. Maybe she's your mom, your aunt, or a neighbor. Find out how things have changed or stayed the same since she was your age. Your list of questions might include some of these:

Did you have a crush on a boy? Who was he, and what did you like about him?

What was your favorite subject in school? What subject was difficult for you?

What sports, hobbies, or clubs were you involved in?

Did you have a best friend when you were my age? What did the two of you do together? Did you ever have a fight? Where is she now?

Who was your favorite teacher? Why?

Did you ever get lonely? What would you do to make yourself feel better?

What did you want to be when you grew up?

How did your family celebrate the holidays? Was there a present you wished for? What special present did you give?

How old were you when you got your period, and how did you feel about it?

Do you remember a time when you were really scared?

What famous people did you admire? Did you hang their pictures up in your room?

What birthday do you most remember? How did you celebrate?

How are things for me different from or the same as when you were growing up?

Words of Wisdom

When you have a heart-to-heart talk, chances are you'll learn something new. Jotting down the information is a good way to remember it. Use these two pages to record your conversation.

Get Moving!

Remember that your body is a work in progress. Try not to focus on how it looks. Your body is in the process of big changes. Instead, think about all the great things your body can do. Start by circling the things below that you can do:

Do yoga

Balance

Wiggle my toes in the sand

Tap a beat

Jump

Swim

Draw

Do a handstand

In-line skate

Hug

Run

Ride a bike

Dance

Ice-skate

Catch fireflies

Jump rope

Do a cartwheel

Climb

Skip

Play badminton

Go sledding

Give a piggyback ride

Play table tennis

Dive

Skateboard

Chase butterflies

Snowboard

Play hide-and-seek

Laugh

Build a snow fort

Take a bow

Walk a dog

Hit a tennis ball

Do a somersault

Play kickball

Walk barefoot

Sing

Catch a softball

Hike

Stretch

Play an instrument

Ski

Kick a soccer ball

Serve a volleyball

Throw a football

Ready? Set? Go!

Are you a couch potato or a jumping bean? Take this quiz to find out. Circle the letter next to the answer that describes you best.

1. You're finally out of the car. You've slapped on some sunscreen and you're ready to hit the beach. The first thing you do is . . .

    a. dip your toes in the surf, spread out your towel, and snooze.

    b. dig in the sand, and build a castle with your brother.

    c. jump waves, swim, and race down the shore after the seagulls.

2. You have 105 TV channels, but today they're all showing reruns. You . . .

    a. watch your six favorite shows again to catch anything you missed seeing the first time.

    b. watch a video and then go outside to practice shooting free throws.

    c. watch TV? Who has time?

3. Good news: a neighborhood friend invited you over. Bad news: your dad can't drive you. You decide to . . .

    a. stay home. No ride? No way! You talk on the phone with your friend instead.

    b. walk over and meet your friend at the park—it's halfway.

    c. hop on your bike and pedal to your friend's house.

4. What a great day you've had camping with your family! Now comes the best part—sitting around the campfire. You volunteer to . . .

> **a.** break up the graham crackers to make s'mores.
>
> **b.** walk around the campsite to find perfect marshmallow sticks for everyone.
>
> **c.** scour the forest to gather armfuls of firewood.

5. Your best friend is sleeping over on Friday! You can't wait to . . .

> **a.** play video games until the sun comes up.
>
> **b.** gather everything you need to make tons of bracelets to give to your classmates.
>
> **c.** turn on your favorite songs and dance the night away.

6. It's Saturday afternoon, and the rain outside means you're staying inside. You decide to . . .

    a. cuddle up with a blanket and read a book from cover to cover.

    b. grab your watercolors and paint a picture for a friend.

    c. rearrange your entire room from top to bottom.

7. Your mom says she wants to do something together, just the two of you. Best of all, you get to pick the activity. You choose . . .

    a. a night on the couch watching family videos of you as a baby.

    b. an afternoon making a scrapbook filled with your family's silliest vacation photos.

    c. a day of swimming at the pool. This time you know Mom will go off the high dive, too!

8. At summer camp, you'd be voted . . .

    a. Bed Bug.

    b. Craft Queen.

    c. Game Girl.

Answers

Mostly **a's**

If you circled mostly a's, you're a girl who knows how to relax. But remember to flex your muscles and work up a sweat for 60 minutes or more each day to keep your body healthy and strong. Find something active that you like to do—then do it! Not into competition? Try a dance class, in-line skating, or swimming to get your heart pounding.

Mostly **b's**

If you circled mostly b's, you're a creative girl with lots of ideas. Use your imagination to find ways to get moving! Play volleyball with friends, start a car-washing business in your neighborhood, or walk through the woods to collect stuff to make a craft. You might also try activities like martial arts or yoga to challenge your body and your brain!

Mostly **c's**

If you circled mostly c's, you're a mover and a shaker. You love to be active, and your muscles love it, too! Keep going, and invite a friend—or even Mom or Dad—to go with you! But don't forget to give yourself a break when needed.

Go Play!

Yes, exercise is important. But it's also fun! Whether you like team sports or solo workouts, getting active is good for you.

I play ....

....

I also like to ....

....

I prefer ☐ team sports ☐ going solo

My favorite time of day to exercise is ....

because ....

....

....

When my heart's pumping, I feel ....

....

....

....

....

After I'm done, I feel

Other ways I get my body moving are

I feel strongest when I

A sport or activity I'd like to learn is

Having Fun

Describe the last time you worked up a sweat and had fun, too.

What's your favorite active way to spend
a Saturday afternoon?

Getting My ZZZs

Get the most out of your day by recharging your body at night. Most girls need at least ten hours of sleep each night. Keeping a bedtime routine helps your body wind down and prepare to rest.

My bedtime on weekdays: .... weekends: ....

Time I begin getting ready for bed: ....

Things I do right before bedtime: ....

....

Hours of sleep I get each night on weekdays: ....

Hours of sleep I get each night on weekends: ....

I sleep with ☐ my bedroom light on

☐ a night-light on

☐ the lights off

I keep my ☐ door closed

☐ door open

☐ door ajar

A drawing of . . .

. . . my *favorite* pajamas

. . . my *favorite* pillowcase

Nightmares

Describe a dream you hope never to have again.

....

....

....

....

....

....

....

....

....

....

....

....

....

Sweet Dreams

Describe a dream you'd like to have again.

....

....

....

....

....

....

....

....

....

....

....

....

....

....

Imagine

The secret to a good night's sleep is to unwind your mind. Create a nighttime version of a daydream. Think of your brain as your own personal television. You are the star and the director. Close your eyes and imagine yourself in a place that makes you happy and calm, doing something that is relaxing.

In my vision, here's . . .

where I am: ....

....

....

....

what I'm doing: ....

....

....

....

what I hear: ....

....

....

....

what I feel:

what I smell:

who is with me:

What I'm Thankful For

Ever tried counting sheep to fall asleep? Boring, huh? Try this instead: count all the things you're thankful for—include the little things. The list will quiet your worries in a hurry.

What's on My Mind

Sometimes our problems are all we can think about. Getting those thoughts out of your head and onto paper will help. Think of this as space to unload what's weighing on your mind.

Here's what's bugging me:

Here's what I'm worried about:

Think Positive

Now, shift your focus. Think about the things that make you feel good.

Here's what I'm excited about:

Here's what I'm looking forward to:

Stay in Control

When you're angry, it's easy for your emotions to take over your actions. But slamming a door, yelling, or sulking will only make matters worse. Talking about things is a better solution. That means expressing yourself calmly—and listening, too.

Think about the last time you were really angry with someone.

What happened that made you angry?

Did you talk to the person who made you angry?

If so, how did you feel about the conversation? Did it go well or was it rocky?

Do you think the other person listened to you?

Did you listen to her?

How do you think the other person felt about the conversation?

Do you wish you could go back and start the conversation over?

If so, what would you do differently?

If you kept your feelings to yourself, what happened?

Time Out

When your temper heats up, stop! Take a break and cool down before you talk about your feelings. Otherwise, you might say something you'll regret. Once you're calm, you'll be ready to have a good conversation.

Check off the ways you blow off steam:

☐ Write in my journal

☐ Take a walk

☐ Play with my pet

☐ Ride my bike

☐ Read a book

☐ Take a bath

☐ Talk to a friend

☐ Take a deep breath and count to 10, 20, or 100—whatever it takes!

☐ Other ....

....

....

Three steps to expressing how you feel:

1. Describe exactly what made you angry.

2. Tell how it made you feel.

3. Try to agree on a way to handle things in the future.

Sometimes talking about feelings brings people closer together. Has this ever happened to you? Describe a time when talking things over not only ended an argument but also made your friendship even stronger.

....

....

....

....

....

....

....

....

....

You're the Expert

You have experience handling life's twists and turns, so don't be surprised by how much you already know. Pretend you're the writer of an advice column, and answer the following letters.

I have a bad habit. I am 12 years old, and I pick at my face. I have tried to stop, but I don't know how. Please help!
—Trying to Stop

Dear Trying to Stop,

I'm nine years old, and I just got glasses. I need them to see the board in class. I am afraid people will laugh at me and call me names. But I like my glasses. What should I do?
—Christy

Dear Christy,

You're the Expert

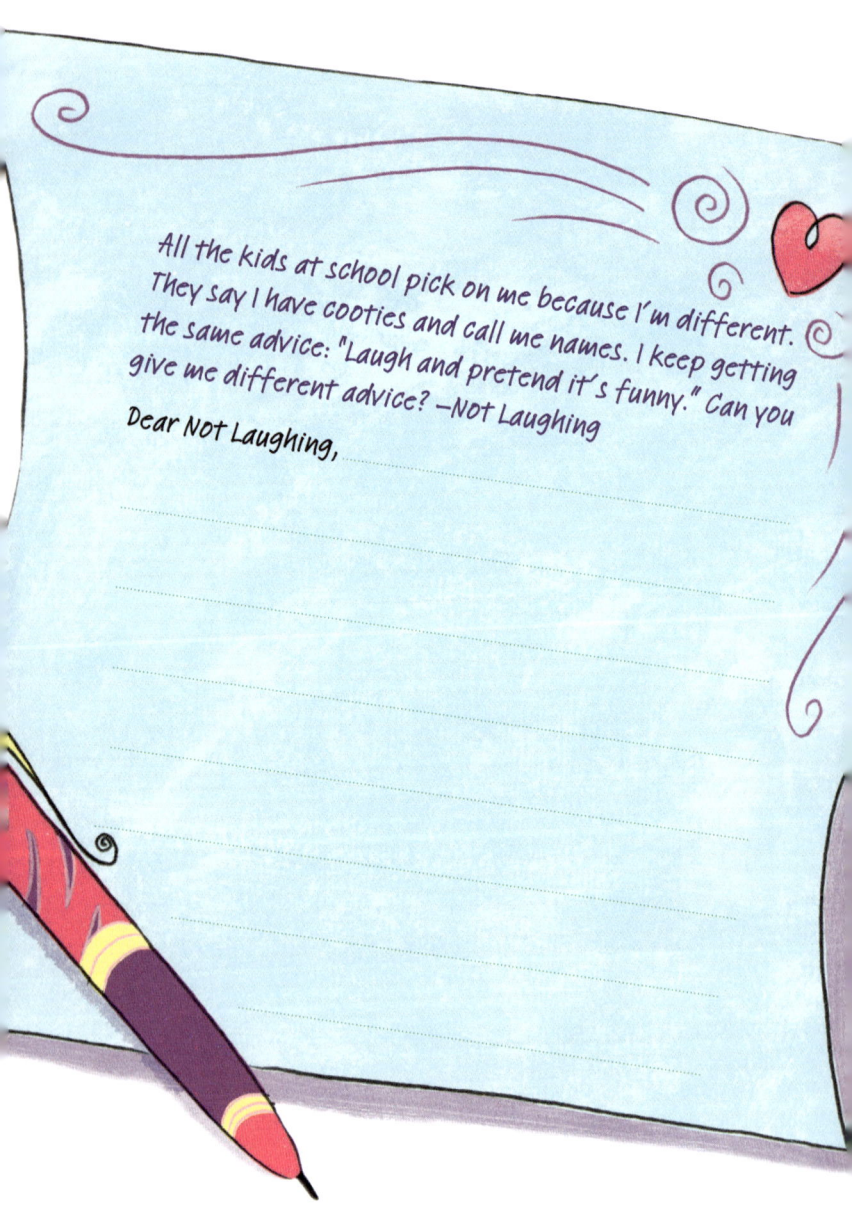

All the kids at school pick on me because I'm different. They say I have cooties and call me names. I keep getting the same advice: "Laugh and pretend it's funny." Can you give me different advice? —Not Laughing

Dear Not Laughing,

I want to be more outgoing. I try to be, but whenever I get around strangers, I just sit there! I'm not shy, but I just can't talk. Please help! —Tongue-Tied

Dear Tongue-Tied,

Dear Me,

Giving others advice sometimes is easier than helping ourselves. But you can be your own best friend, too. When you have a problem, write it down. This will help you pinpoint what's bothering you.

Here's my problem:

Now, step away and pretend the problem belongs to a friend who's seeking your advice. What would you tell her?

Dear friend, here's my advice:

Picture Perfect

Look how far you've come, and imagine where you're going!

A drawing or photo of . . .

. . . me **when I was little**

. . . me **now**

What I might be doing:

....

....

....

....

....

Where I might live:

....

....

....

....

....

A drawing or clipping of how I imagine
I'll look **when I grow up**

Make Wishes

Wishes become goals when you put them on paper. Write your wishes on these stars, and you'll be one step closer to making them come true!

The Feelings Book
Book
Journal

by Dr. Lynda Madison
illustrated by Josée Masse

This journal belongs to

....

....

Published by American Girl Publishing
Copyright © 2005, 2013 by American Girl

Questions or comments? Call 1-800-845-0005,
visit **americangirl.com**, or write to Customer Service,
American Girl, 8400 Fairway Place, Middleton, WI 53562-0497.

Printed in China
13 14 15 16 17 18 19 20 LEO 10 9 8 7 6 5 4 3 2 1

Editorial Development: Therese Maring, Michelle Watkins, Carrie Anton
Art Direction and Design: Chris Lorette David, Camela DeCaire
Production: Tami Kepler, Judith Lary, Paula Moon, Kristi Tabrizi
Illustrations: Josée Masse

Dear Reader,

As you grow up, it's only natural to have many different feelings. These days, you may notice that your feelings change quickly or even that you seem to be juggling several different feelings at once! You may be happy one minute, then down in the dumps, and then go back to feeling happy again.

Strong feelings can make it seem as if you're spinning out of control. But all your feelings—good and bad—can guide you in making smart decisions in your life. Listening to your heart and understanding your emotions can help you be true to yourself and sort out the tricky and sticky situations you face every day.

This companion journal to *The Feelings Book* is filled with checklists, quizzes, and strategies for learning more about your feelings. Fill in the pages. Jot down your thoughts. Take a quiz and answer a few questions. But most of all, think. Have fun learning about yourself, and celebrate the special person you are!

Your friends at American Girl

All About You

You are the only one of you there is.
That makes you a V.I.P.—a Very Important Person! You have special likes, dislikes, hobbies, and activities that make you different from other people. **Take time to remember what makes you unique.**

Some Facts About Me

My name is _____

Sometimes people call me by my nickname, _____

_____

I'm in _____ grade in school.

I live with _____

_____

_____

_____

_____

I enjoy _____

_____

_____

_____

_____

_____

I am good at _____

_____

_____

_____

_____

At school, I like to _____

_____

_____

_____

_____

On weekends, I like to _____

_____

_____

_____

_____

My Friends

One way to look at your connections with others is by making a Friend-o-Gram. Put your name in the middle square and your friends' names in the circles. Add as many circles as you want. Then, draw lines between the names of people who are also friends with each other.

Your Friend-o-Gram is a "snapshot" of the people you feel closest to. It can help you think about how you spend your time. Are there friends you haven't connected with in a while? Give them a call!

(Circle) the words that describe your friends.

My very best friends are

honest

understanding

happy

helpful

smart   kind

supportive

funny

generous

talented

Fill in a name and check all the boxes that apply.

One friend I can really talk to is _____

She's good to talk to because she

☐ cares about me no matter what.

☐ listens without interrupting.

☐ doesn't influence me to do things her way.

☐ understands how I feel.

☐ asks what I think.

☐ has good ideas.

☐ checks with me later to see how things are going.

☐ can keep a secret, but would tell an adult if it was really important.

Some adults I can talk to are

_____ and _____

My Favorite Things

Turn to, or think about, your favorite things when you need to feel comfortable and calm—or when you want to have fun!

Here are some of my all-time favorites:

Holiday _____

Place to travel _____

Color _____

Hobby _____

Clothes _____

TV show _____

Subject in school _____

Actor/Actress _____

Song _____

Movie _____

Stuffed animal _____

Real animal _____

Free-time activity _____

In my house, the room I feel the most comfortable in is

_____

Here's a sketch of this room:

Some ways I like to relax:

☐ Taking a bubble bath

☐ Sitting in a favorite cozy chair

☐ Getting a back rub

☐ Having my hair brushed

☐ Reading a book

☐ Writing

☐ Playing music

☐ Singing

☐ Taking a walk

☐ Talking with a friend

☐ Other _____

_____

_____

Fun Time

Having fun with friends is a great way to relax, have a few laughs, and feel closer.

Here are ten things I like to do with my friends:

1. _____
2. _____
3. _____
4. _____
5. _____

6. _____
7. _____
8. _____
9. _____
10. _____

Long, private talks and quiet conversations with friends are important. (Circle) some of the topics you and your friends talk about.

school

parents

clothes

friends

feelings

sports

movies

boys

upcoming events

books

other_____

other_____

Sleep Time

When you're rested, your mind is sharper than when you're tired. You can concentrate better and you're less likely to feel grumpy. When you miss out on ZZZs, even little troubles can seem worse than they are. How well do you sleep at night?

Most of the time, I

☐ sleep soundly all night.

☐ can't get to sleep.

☐ wake up in the night.

☐ have to drag myself out of bed in the morning.

☐ feel sleepy or tired all day long.

Most girls your age need at least ten hours of sleep every night to feel their best. Keep track for a few nights. Are you getting enough sleep?

	Bedtime	Waking Time	Number of Hours I Slept
Monday			
Tuesday			
Wednesday			
Thursday			
Friday			
Saturday			
Sunday			

What sometimes keeps me awake is _____

_____

_____

Sometimes, instead of going to bed on time, I _____

_____

_____

I might get more shut-eye if _____

_____

_____

What's Your Reaction?

For each situation, pick the reaction that is closest to the way you would probably respond.

1. I thought my mom could take my friends and me to a movie, but it turns out she has to take my brother to track practice. My reaction is to

   a. stomp my foot, cry, and make sure my mother knows I don't appreciate this.

   b. rattle off all the reasons I want to go to the movie, then call my friends to complain.

   c. say it's OK and slink off to my room. There will always be another time.

2. I make the cheerleading squad after three years of hard work! I respond by

   a. turning a handspring right there in the hall. After all, I'm a cheerleader!

   b. telling everyone just how excited I am—even those people who already know.

   c. just smiling. I don't want to call attention to myself right now.

3. I told everyone I'd bring the snacks to the club meeting, but then I leave them at home! My reaction is to

   a. throw my hands in the air and scream, making sure everyone knows what a tragedy this is.

   b. explain to every person I see why I forgot.

   c. quietly promise to bring something special the next time.

4. The big school play is tomorrow and I'm suddenly nervous. I respond by

   a. snapping at people, saying "Leave me alone so I can practice!"

   b. calling all my friends and relatives to rehearse my part.

   c. sitting in my room, going over my lines again and again.

Answers

□ The Nuclear Reactor

If you had mostly **a** answers, your feelings are out there where everyone can see them. It's great that you don't hold things in—people are sure to know where you're coming from! Just take care not to react so quickly that you shut down communication with another person. If you immediately act angry when, underneath it all, you are actually sad, hurt, or scared, other people will get the wrong impression about how you feel. Pay attention to how your behavior affects others. You might not realize that you say or do things that hurt the people around you.

□ The Talker

If you had mostly **b** answers, you let your feelings out by being chatty. Good—talking to others can help you sort through what you are feeling. But be careful to think before you speak, or you could say things you'll regret later. Take time to think about whether you are talking to people who actually want to hear what you have to say, and make sure your words are not hurtful in some way. And don't let your chattiness keep you from figuring out how you really feel.

□ The Private "I"

If you had mostly **c** answers, you may be great at solving problems by yourself, on your own schedule. Or you might be a very quiet or private person who does not want to burden others with your feelings. That can be fine, as long as you don't have a storm of emotions going on inside. If you do, you'll want to get your feelings out where you can take a good look at them, so they don't build up to the point that they make you ill. You might want to talk to others about how you feel so that they can offer help if you need it. Remember, talking to people can help them know that your quietness doesn't mean you're unfriendly.

My Moods

Color in these mood thermometers to show how you've been feeling recently in each of these settings.

At home:

Happiness Thermometer

I'm sky-high happy!

Life is good!

I'm just so-so.

I'm down in the dumps.

Anxiety Thermometer

I'm so tense, I can't move.

I worry a lot.

I barely feel nervous.

I'm as calm as can be.

Anger Thermometer

I'm a one-girl explosion.

I'm starting to boil.

I'm holding things in so that I don't say things I shouldn't.

Everything's A-OK.

Silliness Thermometer

I get giggling about lots of things.

I usually find something to laugh about.

I find it hard to take a joke.

Nothing really seems funny.

At school:

Happiness Thermometer

I'm sky-high happy!

Life is good!

I'm just so-so.

I'm down in the dumps.

Anxiety Thermometer

I'm so tense, I can't move.

I worry a lot.

I barely feel nervous.

I'm as calm as can be.

Anger Thermometer

I'm a one-girl explosion.

I'm starting to boil.

I'm holding things in so that I don't say things I shouldn't.

Everything's A-OK.

Silliness Thermometer

I get giggling about lots of things.

I usually find something to laugh about.

I find it hard to take a joke.

Nothing really seems funny.

When I'm with my friends:

Happiness Thermometer

I'm sky-high happy!

Life is good!

I'm just so-so.

I'm down in the dumps.

Anxiety Thermometer

I'm so tense, I can't move.

I worry a lot.

I barely feel nervous.

I'm as calm as can be.

Anger Thermometer

I'm a one-girl explosion.

I'm starting to boil.

I'm holding things in so that I don't say things I shouldn't.

Everything's A-OK.

Silliness Thermometer

I get giggling about lots of things.

I usually find something to laugh about.

I find it hard to take a joke.

Nothing really seems funny.

Your mood thermometer can help you take stock of how you're feeling about different parts of your life. Keep reading to learn more about your emotions and what you can do about them.

Dealing with Your Feelings

You can learn about yourself by thinking back to times in your life when your feelings were very strong. For each of the emotions on the following pages, try to recall a situation in which you felt that way, what you thought, what you did, and what happened next.

The **Mood Minder** pages help you figure out the best way to deal with the ups and downs of each feeling.

Feeling Happy

Whether you're on top of the world or just satisfied with life, you're probably happy much of the time. If you think about the times you've felt happy—what you were thinking and the things that you did—you may be able to bring back that happy feeling when down.

A time I felt very happy was when _____

_____

_____

_____

I felt happy because _____

_____

_____

When I felt happy, thoughts like this went through my mind:

_____

_____

_____

At the same time, I also felt

- ☐ hopeful.
- ☐ optimistic.
- ☐ excited.
- ☐ awed.
- ☐ joyful.
- ☐ proud.

- ☐ inspired.
- ☐ capable.
- ☐ strong.
- ☐ competent.
- ☐ creative.
- ☐ trusting.

- ☐ safe.
- ☐ silly.
- ☐ anxious.
- ☐ other _____
- _____
- _____

My body reacted to my happiness. I felt this emotion most in my

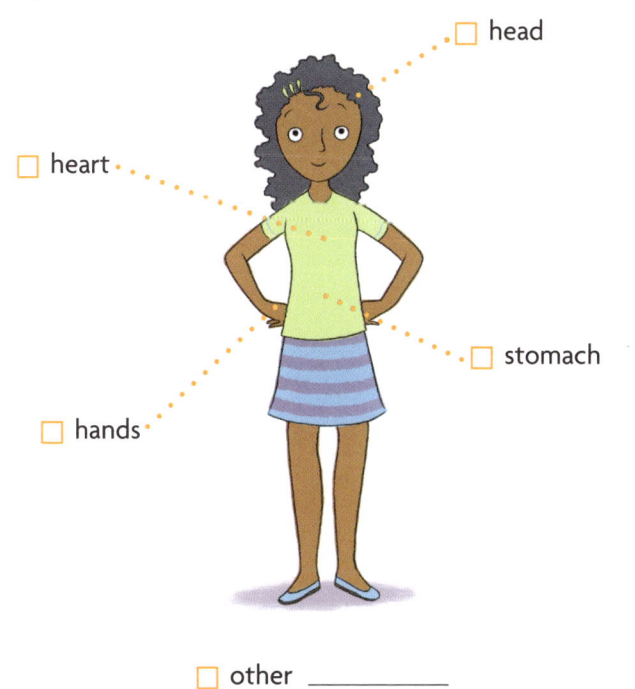

☐ head

☐ heart

☐ stomach

☐ hands

☐ other _____

Mood Minder: I'm Happy

It's important to do things to commemorate your happiest times. Don't miss a chance to pass your happiness on to others, either!

I remember my happy times by

- ☐ looking at photos.

- ☐ taking photos.

- ☐ thinking back through memories.

- ☐ keeping awards and certificates.

- ☐ making a scrapbook.

- ☐ talking about my memories.

- ☐ writing in my journal.

- ☐ keeping souvenirs, such as

_____

_____

- ☐ other _____

_____

_____

Doing nice things for others can help them feel happy.
Surprise! That can make you feel happy, too.

I have done these things for someone else:

☐ Held a door open

☐ Given a gift

☐ Said something nice, such as _____

☐ Had lunch with someone

☐ Read a book to someone

☐ Cleaned

☐ Carried something

☐ Babysat

☐ Volunteered to _____

☐ Sat with someone new at school

☐ Did this special thing: _____

This week, I could make _____ happy by

_____

_____

_____

_____

Feeling Scared

Sometimes it's fun to be scared—like when you're on a roller coaster. When you encounter something genuinely dangerous, such as a mean dog or a speeding car, your body's reaction to feeling scared can actually help you think fast and stay safe.

Other times you may feel frightened about things that aren't really dangerous at all, which isn't fun or helpful! Or you may stay afraid a long time after something has scared you. Learning how you reacted when you were scared in the past may help you be braver the next time around.

I felt scared when _____

_____

_____

_____

I was afraid because I thought something bad would

happen, like _____

_____

_____

My body reacted to my feelings of fear. I felt this emotion most in my

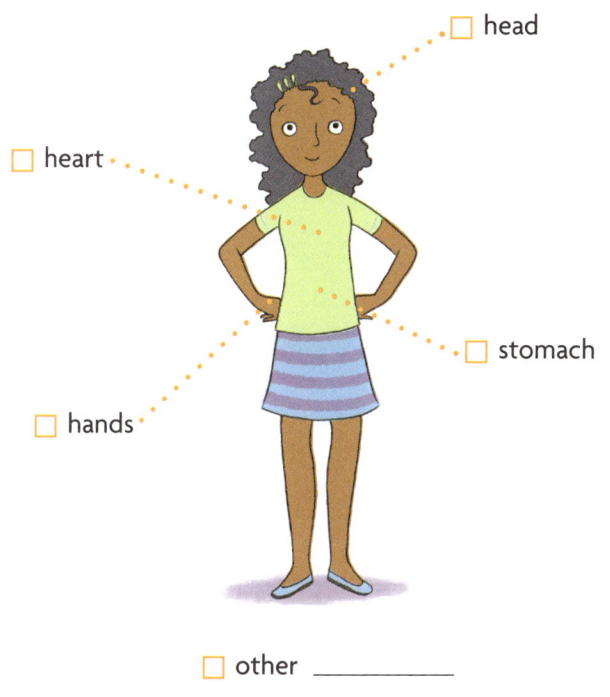

☐ head

☐ heart

☐ stomach

☐ hands

☐ other _____

I reacted to my fear by _____

_____

What helped me feel better was _____

_____

Some other things that scare me are _____

_____

Mood Minder: I'm Scared

When you're scared, the best thing you can do is to calm yourself down so that you can think clearly. Deep, regular breathing allows your body to relax. One way to do this is to count slowly as you breathe deeply. Counting and breathing this way several times will help you control your fear.

When I do deep breathing, I will count to the number ____

A trustworthy friend can also help you calm down. Look for someone who understands why you're afraid but who isn't as scared as you are.

Someone I could talk to is

_____ or _____

Another strategy is to think of something pleasant to take your mind off things. Close your eyes and get a really clear picture in your mind of a comfortable place where you felt safe. Was it the beach, your favorite chair, a cabin in the woods, or someplace else?

A place I felt calm was _____

_____

Here's how this place looked: _____

_____

Sounds I heard when I was there: _____

_____

Scents I smelled there: _____

_____

Exercising your muscles can also help you relax. Put a check-mark next to the activities that work for you.

I can get active by

☐ walking.

☐ jogging.

☐ playing a sport, such as _____

☐ dancing.

☐ swimming.

☐ other _____

_____

Feeling Anxious

Everyone worries now and then. Anxiety can hit you before a big test or performance, or when you think that bad things might happen. Sometimes you may feel uneasy for no particular reason at all. Can you think of a time when you felt anxious? Fill in the blanks and check the boxes below.

I felt anxious when _____

_____

_____

My body reacted to my anxiety. I felt this emotion most in my

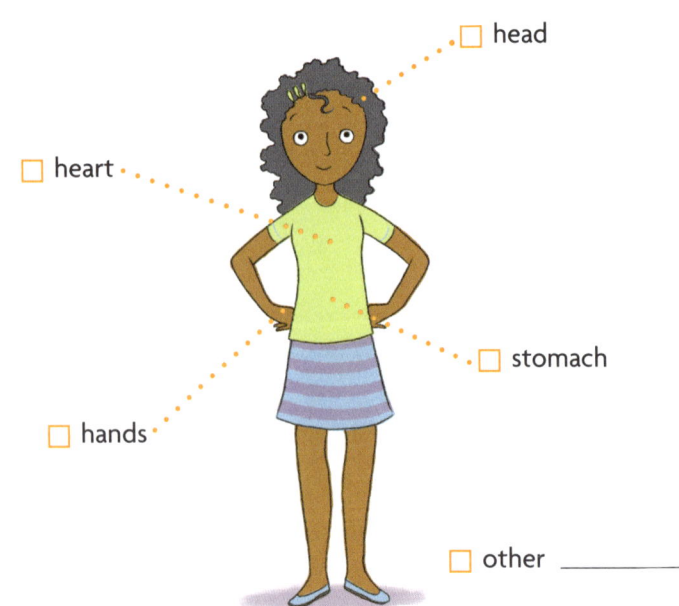

☐ head

☐ heart

☐ stomach

☐ hands

☐ other _____

I worried something bad would happen like _____

_____

_____

_____

I reacted to this feeling by _____

_____

_____

_____

My actions made things

☐ better   ☐ the same   ☐ worse

Other things that make me anxious are _____

_____

_____

_____

_____

Are You a Big Worrier?

Are you as cool as a cucumber or more of a worrywart? Pick the answer that is closest to the way you would respond.

1. I'm doing pretty well in a class until—BOOM!—I get a bad grade on a quiz. I react by

a. realizing that one bad score isn't the end of the world. I'll figure out how to study differently the next time.

b. worrying about whether I'm smart, and thinking I'm sure to fail.

2. My teacher gives me a big part in the school play. I find myself

a. excited about my new adventure, even when the going gets tough. This is fun!

b. thinking of everything that could go wrong along the way, from forgetting my lines to tripping on my final bow.

3. When the seat of my pants rips in math class and everyone sees, I

a. figure this could happen to anyone and realize that my classmates will stop joking soon.

b. just know my life will be awful from here on out. I'll never live this down.

4. I wake up in the night and hear the wind whistling through my window. I decide to

a. close my eyes and think pleasant thoughts until I fall back to sleep.

b. lie there wide-eyed, imagining things much scarier than the wind that could be making that eerie howl.

Answers

If you had mostly **a** answers, you tend to look on the bright side of things and feel confident in most situations. Share your positive outlook with others!

If you had mostly **b** answers, you tend to see mountains where there are only little bumps in the road. Worrying can make things worse than they are. Read on for some strategies to help you regain a positive focus.

Mood Minder: I'm Anxious

Self-confidence is one of the best tools for fighting ner-vousness. You can learn to boost your confidence. Think about a time you kept your worries in check.

One time that I took charge of my worries was when _____

_____

_____

I told myself these positive things: _____

_____

_____

The next time you're worried, see if these thoughts calm you down:

Things will be OK in the end, because

☐ they always have been before.

☐ I have practiced or studied.

☐ I have confidence in myself.

☐ nothing really bad is likely to happen.

☐ I will still be a good person, even if I'm not the best.

☐ my friends will like me no matter what.

☐ other reasons _____

_____

_____

Distracting yourself from your negative thoughts can take your mind off your worries.

One activity I can do to distract myself is _____

_____

Something pleasant I can think about is _____

_____

A friend might tell me, "You don't need to worry because

_____

_____."

Having too much to do can add to your stress, which can make you more anxious. See if you can lighten your daily load of activities.

If I needed to, I could talk to my parents about cutting the following out of my schedule so that I wouldn't be as busy:

_____

_____

_____

_____

Feeling Jealous

People call jealousy a green-eyed monster. We've all met that creature. The monster makes you think you aren't good enough the way you are, but he's wrong. Take charge! Celebrate your life and banish that jealousy monster forever.

I felt jealous when _____

_____

_____

_____

_____

_____

It made me think that _____

_____

_____

_____

_____

_____

My body reacted to my jealousy. I felt this emotion most in my

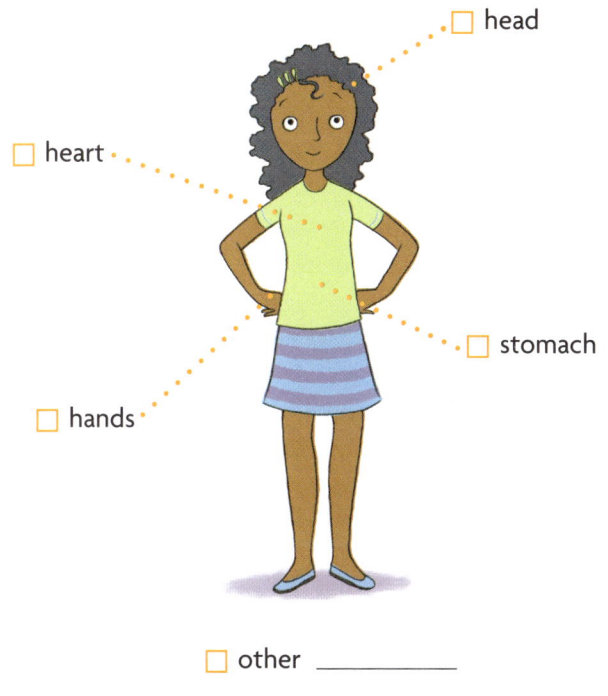

☐ head

☐ heart

☐ stomach

☐ hands

☐ other _____

I reacted by _____

_____

_____

Here's how the situation turned out: _____

_____

_____

Mood Minder: I'm Jealous

To keep from getting jealous, focus on the good things in your life.

I am thankful for people like _____

_____

_____

I am thankful that I'm good at _____

_____

_____

_____

_____

Other things I like about myself and my life are _____

_____

_____

Jealousy can make you do and say things you feel bad about later on. Battle the urge to lash out when you're feeling jealous.

When I feel jealous, I will try not to

☐ make fun of anyone.   ☐ yell.

☐ take away someone's   ☐ cry.
   happiness.
                           ☐ get angry.
☐ do hurtful things.

Making goals can keep you focused on the future instead of on what you think your life is missing right now.

One goal that I have is to _____

Here are two things I can do to help me reach my goal:

1. _____

_____

2. _____

_____

Feeling Disrespected

Sometimes people say or do things to you that just aren't nice. Write about a time when you felt picked on, bullied, or hurt.

I felt really disrespected when _____

_____

_____

_____

_____

My body reacted to my feelings. I felt this emotion most in my

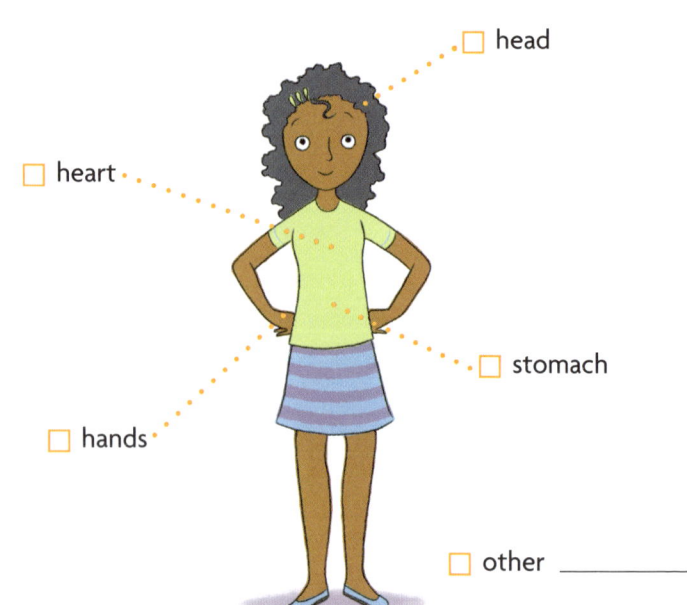

☐ head

☐ heart

☐ stomach

☐ hands

☐ other _____

I reacted to this feeling by _____

_____

_____

_____

_____

Here's how the situation turned out: _____

_____

_____

_____

_____

Deal with Disrespect

If there's someone who regularly makes you feel bad, you shouldn't spend time with her, unless it's to try to improve your relationship. Talking to someone who disrespects you can be scary. A good first step is to write a practice letter that you don't plan to mail or even show to the person. The act of writing it can help you sort out your feelings and help you know what to say when you talk to this person again.

Dear _____ ,

The other day you _____

_____

_____

When that happened, I felt _____

_____

_____

I didn't like feeling that way. I don't know if you meant to do what you did, but would you please not do it again? Thank you very much.

Signed,

_____

When you do talk to the person who's making you feel bad, she may bring up something *you* did that made *her* feel angry or hurt. You may not have meant to hurt her at all. Write another practice letter to sort through how you might respond to her.

Dear _____ ,

I am sorry that I _____

_____

_____

_____

Next time, I'll try to _____

_____

_____

_____

Thanks for letting me know how you felt.

Signed,

_____

Mood Minder: I've Been Dissed!

Don't get down when other people are mean to you. Think about how to respond. First, try to figure out if the person *meant* to be hurtful. Could you be oversensitive about what happened? Check the boxes that could apply.

This person might just have been

☐ busy.

☐ not aware.

☐ in a hurry.

☐ forgetful.

☐ worried about something else.

☐ trying not to look foolish.

☐ simply not thinking about my feelings.

No matter what happened, you are still a good person.
Remind yourself why.

Some things that I like about myself are _____

_____

_____

_____

Some adults I could ask to help me with this situation are

_____

_____

These people love and appreciate me: _____

_____

_____

_____

_____

Feeling Angry

Everyone feels angry at times. You may be mad at another person, at a situation, or even at yourself. When was the last time you felt angry?

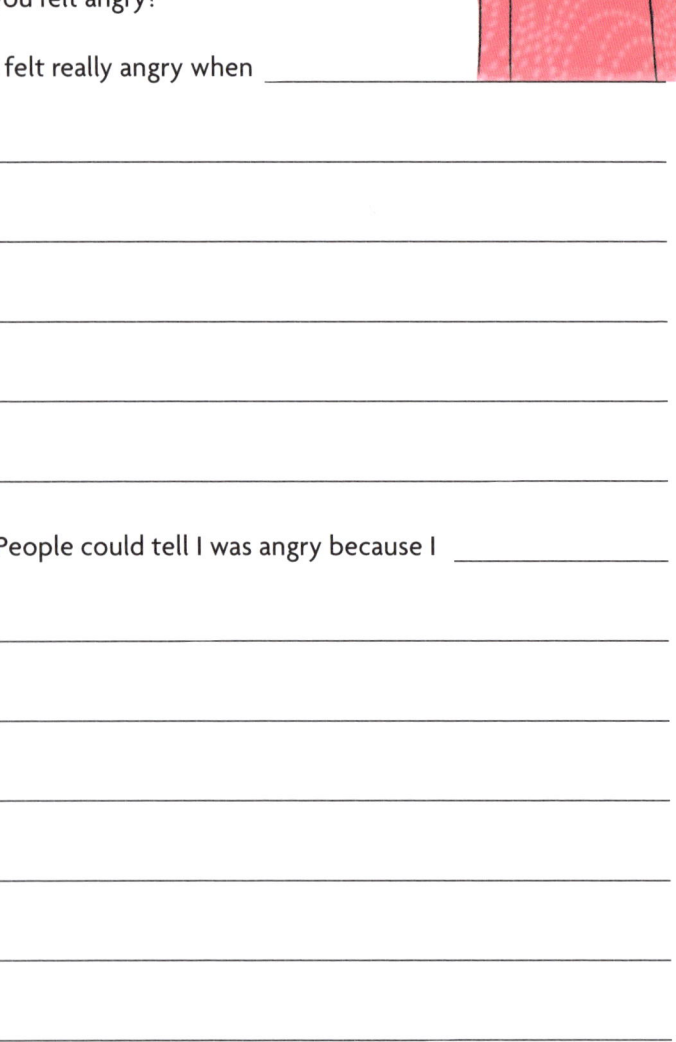

I felt really angry when _____

_____

_____

_____

_____

_____

People could tell I was angry because I _____

_____

_____

_____

_____

_____

_____

Here's how the situation turned out: _____

_____

_____

_____

_____

_____

My body reacted to my anger. I felt this emotion most in my

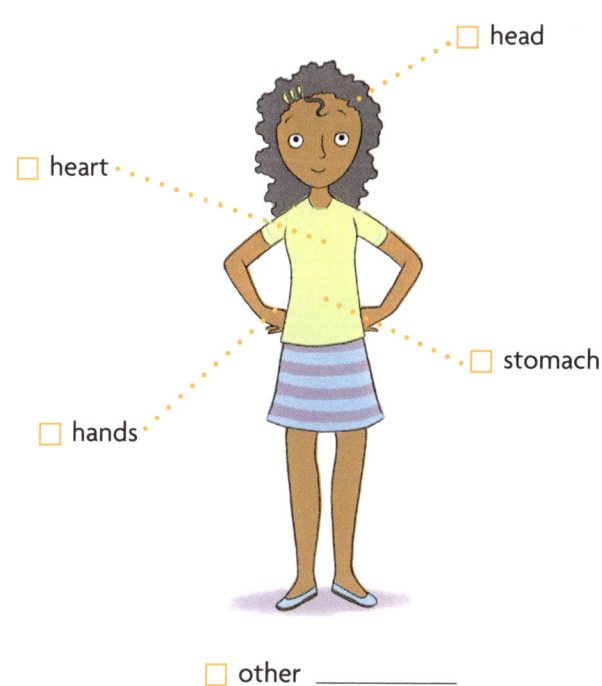

☐ head

☐ heart

☐ stomach

☐ hands

☐ other _____

When you're mad, other feelings can get mixed up with your anger. By recognizing those feelings, you can talk about them, too.

Some feelings I have when I'm angry are

☐ frustration.

☐ confusion.

☐ sadness.

☐ excitement.

☐ jealousy.

☐ anxiety.

☐ embarrassment.

☐ fear.

☐ hurt.

☐ other _____

Are you angry with someone? Writing a practice letter to that person can help you sort out your feelings. The letter isn't meant to be mailed. But writing truthfully about your feelings may help you discover what to do or say to help your situation.

Dear _____ ,

I feel angry right now because _____

_____

When you did that, I felt _____

_____

Maybe you didn't understand how I would feel. Next

time, would you please _____

_____

I'll do my part to make this situation better, too.

I will _____

Thank you.
Sincerely,

_____

Mood Minder: I'm Angry

Lashing out at others can hurt your relationships. It can even get you into trouble. The first thing to do when you feel angry is to keep cool. Take a quick break so that you think before you act. Which "think break" could you take the next time you're angry?

☐ Breathe deeply for a minute.

☐ Count to ten before I take any action.

☐ Walk away for a minute, saying, "I need to think about what just happened."

☐ Find someone to talk to in private about the situation.

You can let your anger out without hurting people or things. Pick one of these safe ways to let off steam, so you don't say or do something you'll regret later.

☐ Punch a pillow   ☐ Dance

☐ Squeeze a ball   ☐ Other _____

☐ Take a walk or a run   _____

☐ Stomp on some   _____
   bubble wrap   _____

After you've calmed down, try talking directly to the person with whom you've been upset. Use this checklist to practice what you need to say.

When I'm angry with someone, I need to

☐ ask to talk for a few minutes.

☐ tell the person I didn't like how things went.

☐ ask if the person realized how I felt.

☐ ask to be treated differently next time.

☐ other _____

_____

_____

_____

_____

_____

_____

Feeling Lonely

Loneliness can happen when you wish you were with someone who's not around. You don't even have to be alone to be lonely. You may feel lonely when you think people around you don't understand or care about you. It can happen even when you are in a big crowd of people. Think about a time when you came down with a wicked case of the lonelies.

I felt lonely when _____

_____

_____

_____

_____

When I was lonely, I wished that _____

_____

_____

_____

_____

_____

This person might have understood how lonely I felt:

_____

Here's how the situation turned out: _____

_____

_____

_____

My body reacted to my loneliness. I felt this emotion most in my

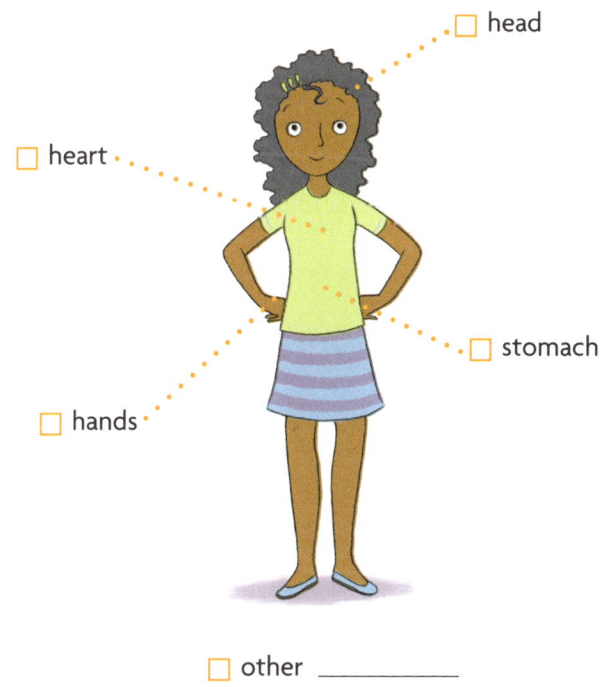

☐ head

☐ heart

☐ stomach

☐ hands

☐ other _____

Alone or Lonely?

Being alone doesn't always make you feel lonely. Take this quiz to see how you tend to react to being by yourself. Pick the answer that is most like how you would respond.

1. All my friends sign up for the soccer team, but I'm not really that interested. I decide to

   a. sign up anyway, so I'm not left out.

   b. do my own thing and figure I'll get together with my friends at other times.

2. My parents are taking me to dinner with my father's boss, who has no kids my age. Before we go, I

   a. complain that it will be boring and I won't know a soul.

   b. decide that I might enjoy talking to someone new. When I'm there, I'll look for a chance to ask questions.

3. It's Friday and I'm ready for fun! But everyone I call has plans for the weekend. I react by

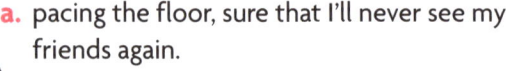

   a. pacing the floor, sure that I'll never see my friends again.

   b. digging out one of my favorite hobbies or curling up in front of a movie I love.

4. I'm at my uncle's wedding, but my entire dance troupe is at a competition I wanted to attend. At the wedding reception, I

a. pout all evening, thinking about what I'm missing.

b. look for other kids my age that I can have fun with. I can even do some dancing right here!

Answers

If you had mostly **a** answers, you enjoy your friends. Great! Just be careful not to depend on them too much for your entertainment and fun. If you keep wishing that you were somewhere else, you'll feel lonelier than you need to feel. Focus on enjoying the here and now, and the time will move along faster. No matter how much fun you think others are having, a little time apart may make all of you appreciate your times together more.

If you had mostly **b** answers, you may prefer to be somewhere else, with people you know and enjoy, but you have a knack for making the best of any situation. Good for you! Being flexible is an important skill to learn. By focusing on the people and activities at your fingertips, you will help everyone have more fun. And guess what? Your independent thinking may be one of the things your friends admire most about you.

Mood Minder: I'm Lonely

Loneliness can make you sad if you focus on what you aren't able to do. Distracting yourself can get your mind off feeling lonely.

What activities could I do the next time I feel lonely?

_____

_____

Sometimes you may feel lonely because you're focusing too much on trying to be with just one or two people.

I do have other friends I haven't seen in a while, such as

_____

_____

It's easy to stay focused on one activity—or one set of friends—but remember that finding new friends might relieve your loneliness.

What new activity or club could I try to meet more people?

_____

_____

If you think too much about someone you miss, you might become a drag on the people you're with now. Stay in the moment. Suggest a fun activity to the people you're with, and you'll have more fun—and feel better, too.

Some fun things I could suggest to the people I'm with right now:

- ☐ Playing a game
- ☐ Watching a movie
- ☐ Going for ice cream
- ☐ Taking a walk
- ☐ Singing together
- ☐ Baking or cooking
- ☐ Listening (or dancing) to music
- ☐ Other _____

_____

_____

Feeling Sad

Sadness is a part of everyone's life. When you are sad, you may cry, become quiet, or act grumpy around others. At times, it can seem tough to do even the simplest things. Think of a time when you felt sad.

I felt sad when _____

_____

_____

My body reacted to my sadness. I felt this emotion most in my

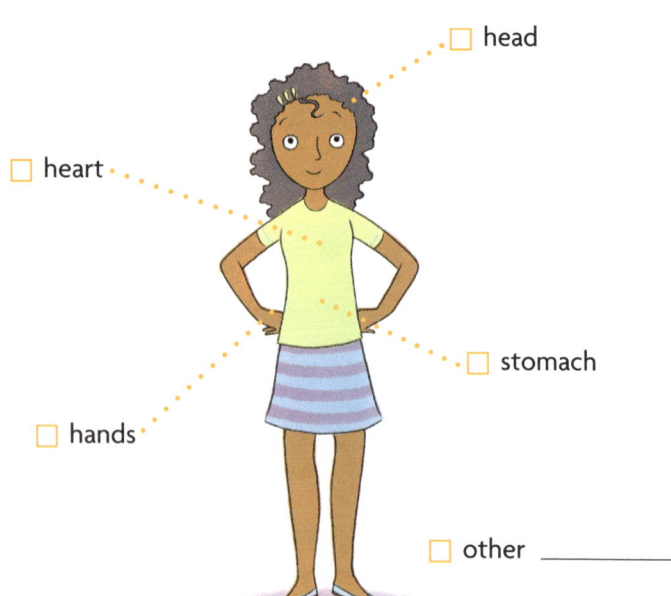

☐ head

☐ heart

☐ stomach

☐ hands

☐ other _____

Some people could tell I was sad because I _____

_____

_____

_____

_____

_____

_____

Something that helped was _____

_____

_____

_____

_____

_____

_____

Mood Minder: I'm Sad

Feeling sad can interfere with friendships, family life, school-work, and activities. One of the best things you can do is tell someone how you feel.

Two people I can talk to are

_____ and _____

Using your artistic talents may help you express your feelings. Which of these art activities would you do when you're feeling down? I would

- ☐ draw.
- ☐ paint.
- ☐ write poetry.
- ☐ dance.
- ☐ sing.
- ☐ keep a journal.
- ☐ sculpt.
- ☐ other _____
- _____

When you are sad, it can seem hard to drag yourself through the day. But getting up and going is always your best defense. How do you like to get your body moving? I like to

- ☐ walk outside.
- ☐ bicycle.
- ☐ run.
- ☐ exercise indoors.
- ☐ swim.
- ☐ dance.
- ☐ play sports.
- ☐ other _____
- _____

You experience life with all five senses. When you feel sad, changing some of the things you see, hear, feel, smell, or taste may help. The next time you're blue, try some of these sensory experiences.

Sight
- Watch an uplifting movie.
- Read an inspiring book.
- Open the curtains and let in the light.

Sound
- Put on some soothing music.
- Call to hear a friend's voice.
- Listen to the birds sing.

Smell
- Breathe in fresh air.
- Smell a flower.
- Notice the aromas of favorite foods cooking.

Touch
- Ask for a hug.
- Have your shoulders rubbed.
- Take a warm bubble bath.

Taste
- Drink some hot tea.
- Share lunch with someone who cares about you.

Sometimes sadness runs deep. If you experience any of the feelings below, show this page to your parents and talk about whether a professional could help you. It may not mean you're depressed, but your sadness may need extra care. Do you

☐ have sadness that lasts more than two weeks?

☐ feel tired all the time?

☐ have difficulty concentrating?

☐ often feel angry or irritable?

☐ not feel like doing things you usually enjoy?

☐ have frequent stomach aches or headaches?

☐ have bad feelings about yourself?

☐ think a lot about death or suicide?*

☐ feel you could hurt yourself or someone else?*

*Note: Even if you didn't check other items, if you checked either of the last two, tell an adult right away and ask to talk to a psychologist or medical doctor.

Feeling Grief

Grief is the mixture of painful emotions you may experience when you lose someone or something you care about. When someone you love dies, you lose a pet, or a good friend moves away, it can feel as though your whole heart aches. The good news is you can let yourself be sad, learn from it, and get through it.

I felt grief when _____

_____

_____

_____

_____

_____

_____

_____

_____

_____

My body reacted to my grief. I felt this emotion most in my

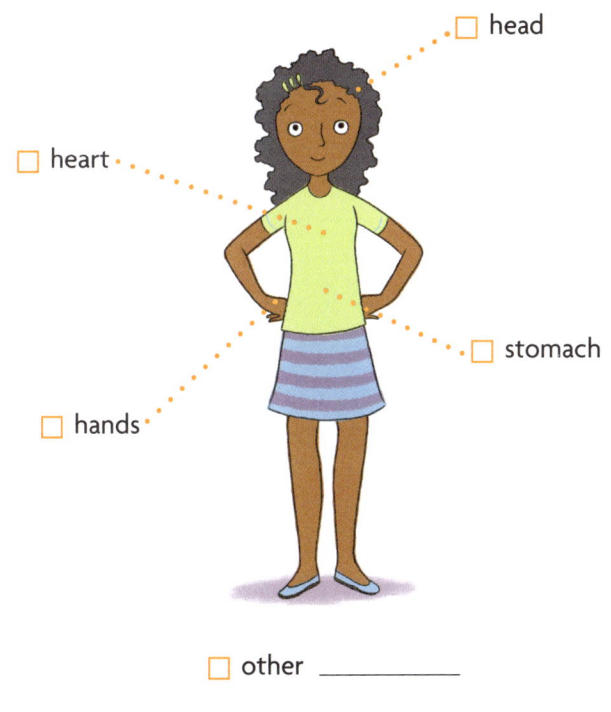

☐ head

☐ heart

☐ stomach

☐ hands

☐ other _____

I talked to _____ about how I felt.

It helped me a little bit when someone said, " _____

_____

_____

_____

_____   _____."

Mood Minder: I'm Grieving

You may experience many feelings as you adjust to your loss. No matter how much it hurts, one of the best things you can do is to talk to someone who understands.

Someone I can talk to about my grief is _____

_____

Keep the person or pet you are grieving for in your heart. Remember something nice that happened with him or her.

One special memory I have is _____

_____

_____

_____

Keeping a special reminder of the person or pet you are missing may help you. Put it on display or keep it someplace where only you will see it.

A special reminder that I have is

_____

_____

_____

Memories can be comforting and pleasant. But dwelling nonstop on sad thoughts will only make you sadder. Remember to direct most of your energy to what you are doing right now, and look forward to good things in the future.

One thing I am looking forward to is _____

_____

_____

_____

_____

_____

_____

Big, Bad Circles

When you're upset, your feelings and actions can go around and around and make you feel worse. Do you recognize these nasty circles of thought?

You **feel** angry because a friend went to the game without you.

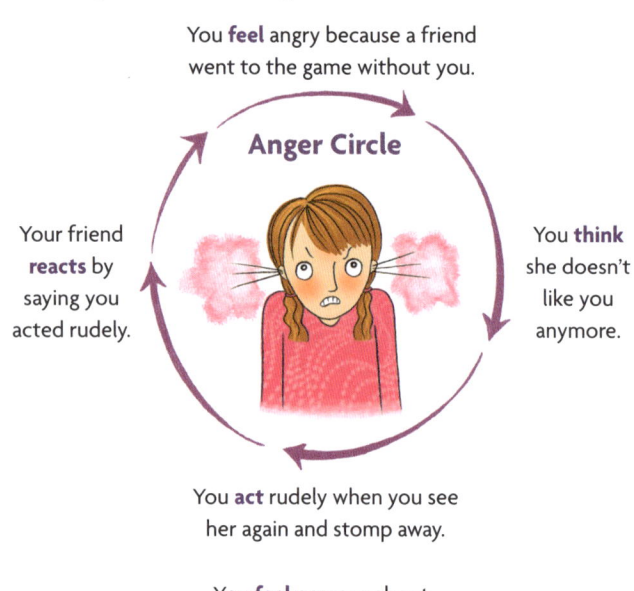

Anger Circle

Your friend **reacts** by saying you acted rudely.

You **think** she doesn't like you anymore.

You **act** rudely when you see her again and stomp away.

You **feel** nervous about giving a school speech.

You **react** by making mistakes you wouldn't have made if you had been calm.

You **think** you are going to mess up.

Anxiety Circle

You **act** jumpy and can't concentrate.

Learn to break the circle!

Can you think of a negative circle you've been in lately?

Here's how I felt:

☐ Sad   ☐ Anxious

☐ Angry   ☐ Other _____

Feeling this way made me think negatively. One thing

I thought was _____

_____

Thinking negatively made me act _____

Here's what I did: _____

_____

Someone reacted to me by _____

_____

_____

This made me

☐ feel the same way I felt to start with, or worse!

☐ think that those negative thoughts about myself
   were right.

☐ act even more negatively than I did in the beginning

Positive Circles

The best way to stop a negative circle is to replace it with a positive circle. Start by changing how you think and act. Eventually this will change how you feel, too. For every negative thought you have about yourself, think about why it might not be true.

Here are some practice thoughts to work on:

If I think, "I'm going to fail this test," I could stop and tell myself, "That's probably not true. I can prepare by

_____

_____."

If I think, "I'm not likable," I could stop and tell myself, "That's probably not true. Not everyone may like me, but my friends like me because

_____

_____."

If I think, "Nobody wants to spend time with me," I could stop and tell myself, "That's probably not true. I could call these people:

_____."

With a little practice, you can create positive circles wherever you are. Try it!

You **feel** good at the moment.

You **think**, "I'm a good person. People like me, and I'm fun to be around."

You **act** relaxed and are pleasant to people. You are interested in others.

Others **react** by wanting to be with you and saying positive things about you.

Confidence Circle

And the circle keeps going around—this time in a good direction!

Congratulations!

Using your journal, you've learned many ways to feel better when you are upset. Look through the list below and mark some of your favorite strategies:

When I'm upset, I can

☐ tell myself this positive thing: _____

_____

_____

_____

_____

☐ talk to _____

    or _____

☐ get moving—walk, play a sport, or dance.

☐ express myself creatively through writing, music, or another art form.

☐ change my surroundings.

☐ help someone else by _____

_____

_____

_____

☐ take care of myself—eat healthily, get enough sleep, and have fun.

☐ relax!

A Letter to Myself

Remember, you are the only **you** there is. You have unique strengths. If you like who you are, others will like you, too. Be nice to yourself! Imagine that you are your own best friend, and write yourself a letter. Give it a read whenever you need a boost.

Dear _____,
(your name)

Even though you feel down sometimes, here are some positive words that describe you—and I'm checking all that apply:

- ☐ Happy
- ☐ Funny
- ☐ Kind
- ☐ Caring
- ☐ Sweet
- ☐ Sensitive
- ☐ Creative
- ☐ Clever
- ☐ Smart

- ☐ Organized
- ☐ Coordinated
- ☐ Studious
- ☐ Level-headed
- ☐ Calm
- ☐ Attractive
- ☐ Nice hair
- ☐ Pretty eyes
- ☐ Good reader

- ☐ Talented
- ☐ Brave
- ☐ A leader
- ☐ Hardworking
- ☐ Good speaker
- ☐ Good writer
- ☐ Musical
- ☐ Generous

I know other good things about you, too. For instance,

_____

_____

Other people like you, too. Someone once said this

nice thing about you: " _____

_____

_____."

You are also a thoughtful person. For example, it was

really nice when you _____

_____

_____

You're a good person and a good friend!

Love, _____

Journal Pages

Now you know a lot about
managing your emotions. Don't stop paying
attention to how you feel. Keep sharing
what you think, and remember to use your
Mood Minders. Use the rest of your journal
to record what happens during your days.
Have fun!

My Journal Entry

Date _____

Today a

☐ crazy ☐ great ☐ irritating

☐ funny ☐ sad ☐ goofy

☐ embarrassing ☐ scary ☐ happy

thing happened. It went like this: _____

_____

_____

_____

_____

On the happiness scale, today was

☐ soaring. ☐ good. ☐ just so-so. ☐ the pits.

I'll tell you why: _____

_____

_____

_____

_____

_____

Here's something I could do about the way I feel: _____

_____

_____

_____

Other thoughts about the day: _____

_____

_____

_____

_____

_____

_____

_____

_____

_____

_____

_____

My Journal Entry

Date _____

Today a

☐ crazy   ☐ great   ☐ irritating

☐ funny   ☐ sad   ☐ goofy

☐ embarrassing   ☐ scary   ☐ happy

thing happened. It went like this: _____

_____

_____

_____

_____

On the happiness scale, today was

☐ soaring.   ☐ good.   ☐ just so-so.   ☐ the pits.

I'll tell you why: _____

_____

_____

_____

_____

_____

Here's something I could do about the way I feel: _____

_____

_____

_____

Other thoughts about the day: _____

_____

_____

_____

_____

_____

_____

_____

_____

_____

_____

_____

My Journal Entry

Date _____

Today a

☐ crazy   ☐ great   ☐ irritating

☐ funny   ☐ sad   ☐ goofy

☐ embarrassing   ☐ scary   ☐ happy

thing happened. It went like this: _____

_____

_____

_____

_____

On the happiness scale, today was

☐ soaring.   ☐ good.   ☐ just so-so.   ☐ the pits.

I'll tell you why: _____

_____

_____

_____

_____

_____

Here's something I could do about the way I feel: _____

_____

_____

_____

Other thoughts about the day: _____

_____

_____

_____

_____

_____

_____

_____

_____

_____

_____

_____

My Journal Entry

Date _____

Today a

☐ crazy   ☐ great   ☐ irritating

☐ funny   ☐ sad   ☐ goofy

☐ embarrassing ☐ scary   ☐ happy

thing happened. It went like this: _____

_____

_____

_____

_____

On the happiness scale, today was

☐ soaring.   ☐ good.   ☐ just so-so.   ☐ the pits.

I'll tell you why: _____

_____

_____

_____

_____

_____

Here's something I could do about the way I feel: _____

_____

_____

_____

Other thoughts about the day: _____

_____

_____

_____

_____

_____

_____

_____

_____

_____

_____

My Journal Entry

Date _____

Today a

☐ crazy   ☐ great   ☐ irritating

☐ funny   ☐ sad   ☐ goofy

☐ embarrassing   ☐ scary   ☐ happy

thing happened. It went like this: _____

_____

_____

_____

_____

On the happiness scale, today was

☐ soaring.   ☐ good.   ☐ just so-so.   ☐ the pits.

I'll tell you why: _____

_____

_____

_____

_____

_____

Here's something I could do about the way I feel: _____

_____

_____

_____

Other thoughts about the day: _____

_____

_____

_____

_____

_____

_____

_____

_____

_____

_____

_____

My Journal Entry

Date _____

Today a

☐ crazy   ☐ great   ☐ irritating

☐ funny   ☐ sad   ☐ goofy

☐ embarrassing   ☐ scary   ☐ happy

thing happened. It went like this: _____

_____

_____

_____

_____

On the happiness scale, today was

☐ soaring.   ☐ good.   ☐ just so-so.   ☐ the pits.

I'll tell you why: _____

_____

_____

_____

_____

_____

Here's something I could do about the way I feel: _____

_____

_____

_____

Other thoughts about the day: _____

_____

_____

_____

_____

_____

_____

_____

_____

_____

_____

_____

My Journal Entry

Date _____

Today a

☐ crazy   ☐ great   ☐ irritating

☐ funny   ☐ sad   ☐ goofy

☐ embarrassing   ☐ scary   ☐ happy

thing happened. It went like this: _____

_____

_____

_____

_____

On the happiness scale, today was

☐ soaring.   ☐ good.   ☐ just so-so.   ☐ the pits.

I'll tell you why: _____

_____

_____

_____

_____

_____

Here's something I could do about the way I feel: _____

_____

_____

_____

Other thoughts about the day: _____

_____

_____

_____

_____

_____

_____

_____

_____

_____

_____

_____

All done?
You can make extra journal pages
in any notebook you have.
Keep on writing!

Write to us!

At American Girl, we love hearing from girls just like you. Tell us what you think of *The Feelings Book Journal*! Send us your questions and ideas.

Write to us at:
Feelings Book Editor
American Girl
8400 Fairway Place
Middleton, WI 53562

Here are some other
American Girl books you might like:

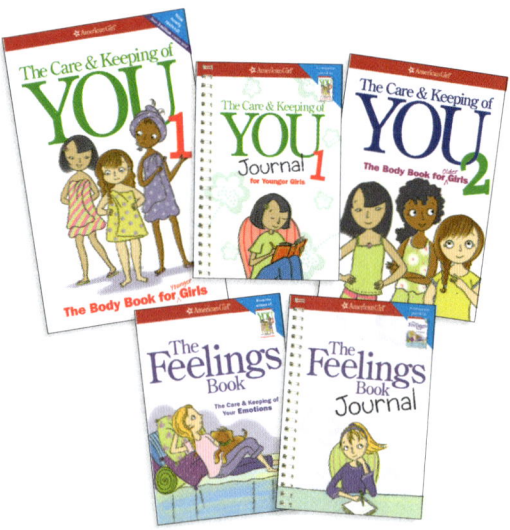

American Girl offers a family of body and mind books for girls just like you to turn to for advice about growing up. Millions of younger girls have used *The Care & Keeping of You 1* to get started, as well as it's companion, *The Care & Keeping of You 1 Journal*. *The Feelings Book* along with this companion journal help you handle the new emotions you may be feeling. And when you're ready, *The Care & Keeping of You 2: The Body Book for Older Girls* will help guide you through the physical, emotional, and social changes that you may need help understanding.

The Care & Keeping of YOU 1

The Body Book for younger Girls

by Valorie Lee Schaefer

Cara Natterson, MD, medical consultant

illustrated by Josée Masse

★ American Girl®

Dear American Girl,

I am a preteen, and all of a sudden growing up is becoming a big and important issue. I don't feel comfortable talking to my parents about it. I feel like it's too personal to talk to an adult about.

Please help me.

Growing Up

Published by American Girl Publishing
Copyright © 1998, revised ed. © 2012 by American Girl

Questions or comments? Call 1-800-845-0005, visit **americangirl.com,** or write to Customer Service, American Girl, 8400 Fairway Place, Middleton, WI 53562-0497.

Printed in China
13 14 15 16 17 18 19 20 LEO 10 9 8 7 6 5 4 3 2

All American Girl marks are trademarks of American Girl.

Editorial Development: Michelle Nowadly Watkins, Andrea Weiss, Carrie Anton, Mary Richards, Barbara Stretchberry
Creative Director: Kym Abrams
Managing Art Director: Marilyn Dawson, Camela Decaire
Design: Ingrid Hess, Camela Decaire
Production: Judith Lary, Sarah Boecher, Tami Kepler, Jeannette Bailey
Medical Consultant: Lia Gaggino, MD, Cara Natterson, MD

Cataloging-in-Publication data available from the Library of Congress

Letter to You

When you were little, your parents took care of you. Now that you're older, you're taking over a lot of that responsibility, and it's not always easy to know what to do or how to ask for help.

It's a struggle for any girl to ask questions when she's dying of embarrassment and digging for the right words to use.

So, what can you do? For starters, you need to get information. The more you know about your body, the less confusing and embarrassing growing up will seem—and the easier it will be to talk about.

We hope the head-to-toe advice in this book will give you the words to start a conversation with your parents or other adults you trust. Your parents were there for you when you were little, and they can still be there for you now. If you speak up, no matter how awkward you feel, your confidence and spirit will grow right along with your body!

Your friends at American Girl

Contents

9 YRS. —

7 YRS. —

5 YRS. —

3 YRS. —

1 YR. —

Body Basics

With your body on the brink of some pretty big **changes,** it's time to start taking control of your **health** and **well-being.** This section introduces you to the **basic facts** about **puberty** and reminds you to take care of yourself, inside and out.

The Basic Facts

Taking care of your body is a lifelong job. And it's more important than ever right now, while you're going through big changes.

The Changes Ahead

Puberty is a special time of growth and change. Everybody goes through it. It begins for most girls between the ages of 8 and 13, and it ends when your body has reached its adult height and size, around ages 15 to 17.

During puberty you'll grow up and out, and not all parts will grow at the same rate. At times you may look and feel like a puppy whose paws are too big for its body! You'll notice changes in your skin, hair, breasts, and other parts of your body. And you'll experience new emotions, too. All of these changes are caused by hormones, chemicals your body produces to change you from a young girl to a woman.

Are you the shortest girl in your class, or do you tower above everyone, including the boys? All of that could change in the very near future!

Get Informed

You may be eager for your body to get growing, or you may be worried about the changes ahead. But the more you know about your body, the less surprised you'll be. So get the facts. Reading books like this one is a great start. You'll find answers to questions you may have never even thought of!

But no book is a substitute for talking to your parents, your doctor, or other adults you trust— people whose job is to take care of you. No question is too silly or too embarrassing to ask. Remember, the grown-ups in your life were once your age, too, and have experience and wisdom to share with you.

Celebrate YOU

Remember that your body is
a work in progress. Try not to
focus on what it *looks like*.
Instead, think about all the great
things your body can *do*.

You may feel like you don't have any control over your growing body. Not true! You *are* the boss when it comes to taking care of these basics.

Pay Attention

Your body is talking to you. Can you hear it? Learn to tune in to your body and hear its warnings. If your body says it's thirsty, drink more water. If your body is tired, give it a rest.

Keep Clean

All that hard work your body's doing to grow up means you'll need to bathe or shower more often, especially if you're active in sweaty sports.

Exercise

You don't have to be an Olympic athlete to be healthy. Just put down that video game, get off the couch, and get moving! Skate to a friend's house or dance to your favorite music. The busier you keep your body, the better you'll feel.

Just Don't

No girl can look and feel her best with cigarette smoke, alcohol, or drugs in her body. Though drinking and smoking may seem "grown-up," the truth is, they're bad for your health. And drugs can destroy your family and future. A smart girl turns her back and walks away from so-called friends who put pressure on her to "just try it."

PRIVATE

Your body is yours and yours alone. You have the right to protect it and keep it private from anyone—family, friend, or stranger. If any person touches you in a way that makes you feel uncomfortable, tell an adult you trust immediately. You should never keep a secret that is harmful to you or protect anyone who is hurting you.

If you feel good about yourself on the inside,
you'll sparkle on the outside!

Most images of women you see on TV just aren't realistic. Look around. Real women's bodies look like your mom's, your teacher's, your next-door neighbor's.

Compare? No Fair!

It's tempting to compare yourself to the girls you see on TV and in magazines and movies. But hold on! Is it fair to measure yourself against made-in-Hollywood images created by makeup artists and photo wizards? No way! You don't need to measure yourself against anyone at all, including friends or other girls at school. You're you—a one-of-a-kind original—and you're beautiful in your own unique way.

It Isn't a Race

A girl's body changes to a woman's body gradually, not overnight. Each girl develops at her own rate. Even sisters don't develop at the same rate. And it's important to remember that growing up isn't a race. There are no prizes for being the first—or last—girl to lose all her baby teeth or to wear a bra. Trust that your body will do all the right things at the time that is right for you.

What's on the Inside

The most attractive girl in the room isn't the girl with the thinnest waist or the fairest face. It's the girl who brims with self-confidence. She's the one who stands head and shoulders above the crowd. That girl can be you. It all starts with a positive attitude.

To have a positive attitude, try to see yourself as a whole person shining through your features. Focus on what's best about you and refuse to hunt for negatives. Don't doubt yourself—be proud of yourself for doing your best.

Kindness Counts

As your body is growing and changing, be kind to yourself. And remember to be kind to other girls, too. They want to feel good about themselves, just like you do.

13

Heads Up!

Let's take it from the top, with tips for handling your **hair,** sound advice on **ears,** and bright tips for bright **eyes.** Learn how a healthy **mouth** makes for a great grin. Brush up on tooth, gum, and **braces** basics. Finally, get the scoop on the skin you're in so you can put your best **face** forward!

Hair Care

Start your everyday grooming routine right at the top with clean, shiny, freshly combed hair.

Do Keep It Clean

As you get older, your hair may get more oily. Keep it clean by washing it regularly. For most girls this means several times a week. If you're an active athlete, or if you have very oily hair, you may want to wash it every day. Use a mild shampoo that's made for your hair type. If your hair tangles easily, use a conditioner to smooth it out.

Do De-chlorinate

If you're a swimmer, rinse the pool water out of your hair after every dip. Chlorine can be very drying, and other chemicals can turn blond hair green. You can buy special shampoos made for swimmers, but regular shampoo often works just as well.

Do Wash Tools

Make sure your brushes and combs are as squeaky-clean as your hair. About once a week, give them a swish in warm, soapy water—you can use shampoo or even mild dish detergent. Rinse thoroughly.

Don't Mangle Tangles

While your hair is still wet, use a wide-tooth comb to detangle small sections. Start with the ends first and work your way up. If you hit a rough spot, don't yank! Gently work the comb through your hair.

Do Use the Right Tools

Some hair-care tools can damage your hair and scalp. Choose a brush with a rubber base and round-tipped bristles. Never use a brush on wet hair, which is weaker than dry hair— the brush stretches the hair out and can cause it to break. Use a wide-tooth comb instead.

Don't Share

Sharing is a good thing, except when it comes to hair tools. Don't borrow combs and brushes from friends or family members, and don't lend them yours. It isn't stingy—it's good hygiene.

Don't Overheat

Blow-dryers, straightening irons, and curling irons can really dry out your hair. If possible, let your hair dry naturally. If you use a blow-dryer, use the warm or cool setting. Don't use straightening irons and curling irons every day—save them for special occasions.

Hair Scare!

When hair-raising horrors happen to you, here's how to handle them.

Getting Gum Out

Uh-oh! Somehow you've managed to get a big, juicy wad of gum in your hair. Before you reach for the scissors, try this age-old trick. Spread a glob of peanut butter on the gum. Work the peanut butter through your hair until the gum comes out. The peanut butter will wash out with a regular shampoo.

Greasy Hair

During puberty, your oil glands get more active. For some girls this means greasy hair. If the roots of your hair look oily almost every day, you may have to shampoo more often.

Dandruff

Does your scalp feel dry and itchy? Are your shoulders covered with flakes of skin, making your dark-colored shirts look like they're sprinkled with snow? You may have a case of *dandruff*, a very common condition that's easy to treat. Try a dandruff shampoo from the drugstore. If drugstore shampoos don't work, ask your doctor for something stronger.

Hair products such as mousse, sprays, and gels can cause flakes and itching from buildup. Shampoo regularly to remove the buildup.

EEK—a Louse!

Head lice are a common problem among schoolkids everywhere. These tiny wingless parasites thrive in thickets of human hair. They bite the scalp, leaving tiny sores that itch like crazy. Worst of all, a single louse can lay hundreds of eggs, called nits, right on your head! If lice are on the loose at your school, take action to protect yourself. Don't share combs and brushes with friends. Don't swap hats, hair bands, or headphones, and don't trade pillows at sleepovers.

If you suspect unwelcome guests on your head, see your doctor or school nurse. They know a louse when they see one. Live lice are small and gray, and move around. Nits look like white grains of sand and are often found along the hairline above the neck and behind the ears. If it turns out you have lice, your parents can buy delousing products at the drugstore and follow the instructions carefully to get rid of the lice completely and to keep them from coming back.

Nits "glue" themselves to hair and can be hard to get out. A special fine-tooth "nit comb" can help pick out the nits.

Ears

Ears are easy to care for. They need just a little help from you to stay healthy inside and out—so every sound you hear will be crystal clear.

Squeaky Clean

Your ears get washed every time you shampoo or shower. In most cases, that's all the cleaning they need. Shake your head to remove excess water, and use a towel, washcloth, or cotton swab to wipe off the outer part of your ears. NEVER stick a pointy object into your ears—not even a cotton swab. You could do serious damage to your eardrums or canals. Ear wax, that sticky yellowish stuff inside, is something you're supposed to have. Wax acts as a sort of flypaper, sticking to dirt and preventing it from traveling into your ear canal. You can, however, have too much wax. If your ears feel plugged, talk to your doctor to find out a safe way to get the gobs out.

Pierced Ears

If you want to get your ears pierced, go to a professional who uses clean, sterile equipment. Allow two to three months for the holes to heal before you change earrings. Clean your newly pierced ears daily with a cotton swab dipped in rubbing alcohol. Redness, itching, or oozing near the hole may be a sign of infection. If this happens, call your doctor for advice.

Headphones

It's OK to turn on the music and tune out the world, but don't turn up the volume! Over time, exposing your ears to loud noise can damage your hearing. Take this test. If someone stands next to you and can hear sound coming out of your headphones, the volume is too loud.

Many girls are allergic to the metals used in cheap earrings. To be safe, look for surgical steel, sterling silver, or 14-karat gold.

Swimmer's Ear

If you spend your summers at the lake or in the pool, you're a good candidate for swimmer's ear. This is an infection that occurs when bacteria in the water get into your ear and grow, causing a painful earache. The best way to prevent swimmer's ear is to dry out the ears and disinfect the canals. Follow these steps:

1. After you swim, dry your ears thoroughly with a towel.

2. Mix 1 teaspoon rubbing alcohol with 1 teaspoon white vinegar. Ask a parent to put a few drops in each ear. The alcohol helps dry out the ear, and the vinegar kills bacteria.

3. If you have ear pain, especially when you tug on your ear, see a doctor.

Eyes

It's a good idea to have your vision checked every year at school or your doctor's office. If you have trouble seeing things far away, such as a blackboard, you may be nearsighted. If you have trouble reading up close, you may be farsighted.

Be on the Lookout

Many girls don't notice problems with their eyesight until they have to do a lot of reading or looking at the chalkboard in school. This is often between third and fifth grades. You may need glasses if you have:

• headaches while or after you've been reading.

• trouble seeing objects at a distance or up close.

• double vision not caused by just crossing your eyes.

Eye Exams

If you're having difficulty with your eyes, have them checked by an eye-care professional. Even if you aren't having problems, doctors say you should have an exam by the time you've begun to read. It's important to check for early signs of disease. At the exam, you'll be asked to read a special chart up close and at a distance. The doctor will look at your eyes through a kind of microscope and may put drops in your eyes to dilate, or enlarge, your pupils. This helps the doctor see inside your eyes, and it doesn't hurt at all.

"I just got glasses. I was worried everybody would make fun of me, but I realized that after a while, no one will remember what I look like without them!"

Courtney

You're Not Alone

Your vision may continue to change during the time you're in grade school and level off when you reach your teens. If you're one of the first to get glasses, you may feel like the loneliest girl in the world. But peek around your classroom in a couple of years, and you'll find that you've got lots of company!

Glasses

Glasses are convenient and easy to care for. They come in lots of fun colors and styles. Some girls think of their eyeglasses as fashion accessories!

Contact Lenses

Contact lenses change the way you see without changing the way you look. But they're also expensive and require daily care and cleaning. Some girls don't feel ready for this responsibility.

Eye Protection

Your eyes can burn just like your skin. Wear sunglasses at the pool or beach or on the ski slope to protect your eyes from ultraviolet rays. Look for shades marked "UVA/UVB pro-tection." Don't stare into the sun, and never look directly at a solar eclipse, even with sunglasses.

Mouth

A smile is an invitation that you wear on your face. It says, "I'm a girl you want to know!" Make sure your smile is a warm greeting and a sign of good health by brushing up on the basics.

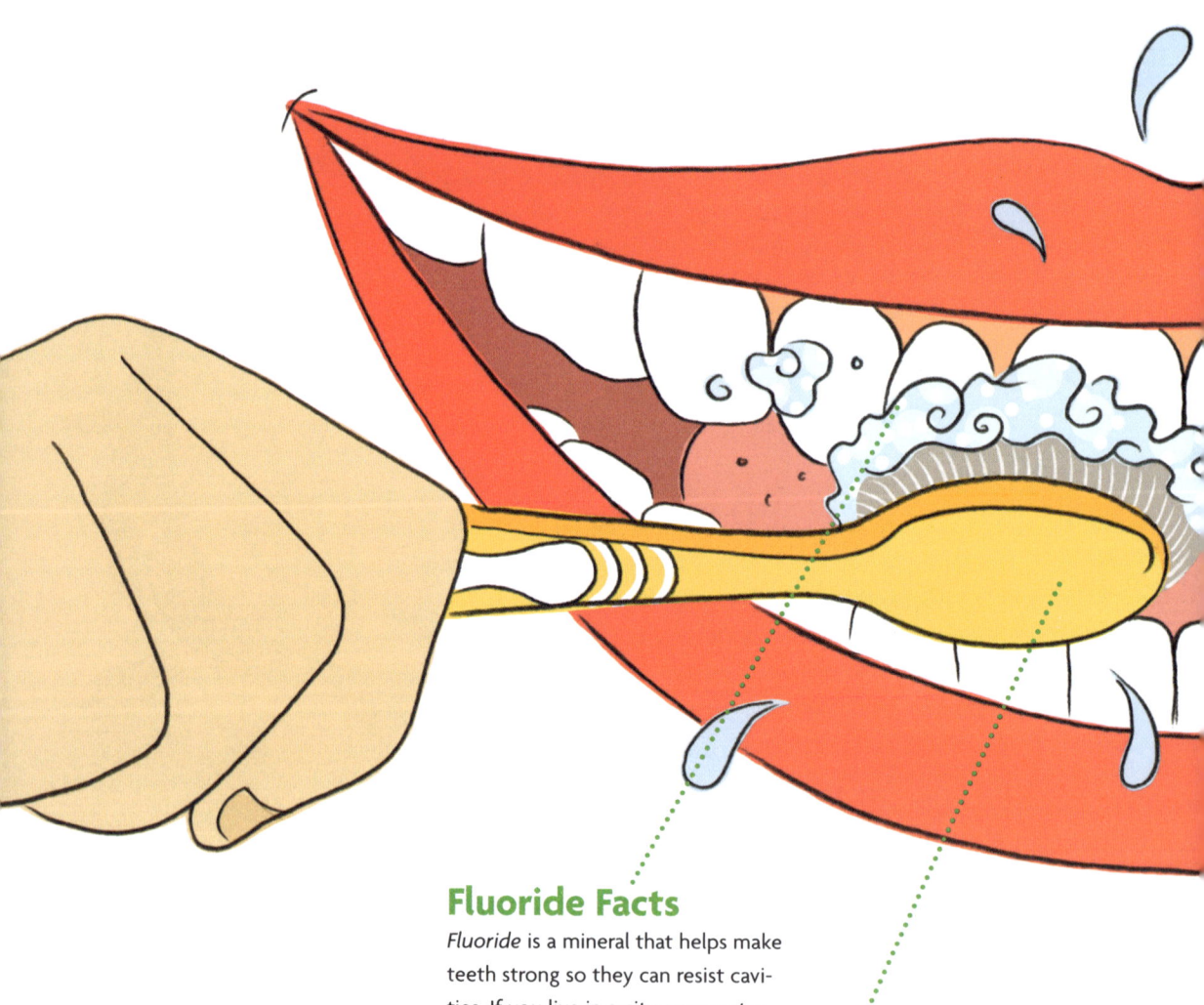

Fluoride Facts

Fluoride is a mineral that helps make teeth strong so they can resist cavities. If you live in a city, your water probably has some fluoride in it. Make sure your toothpaste does, too. And you don't need a huge gob of paste to get the job done—just a squirt about the size of a pea.

Toothbrush Basics

Choose a small toothbrush with soft, rounded bristles. Replace your brush every two to three months, or as soon as the bristles get droopy. Bent bristles won't clean your teeth properly, and they can harm your gums.

Daily Duty

Plaque is a gooey bacterial film that forms on your teeth. It can cause cavities and gum disease. Attack plaque! Brush your teeth first thing in the morning and at bedtime. Try to brush after eating, too. Pack a toothbrush in your backpack and slumber party kit so you won't be tempted to skip. Do it every day, the right way. No fair just swishing the toothpaste around a little! Correct brushing takes minutes, not seconds.

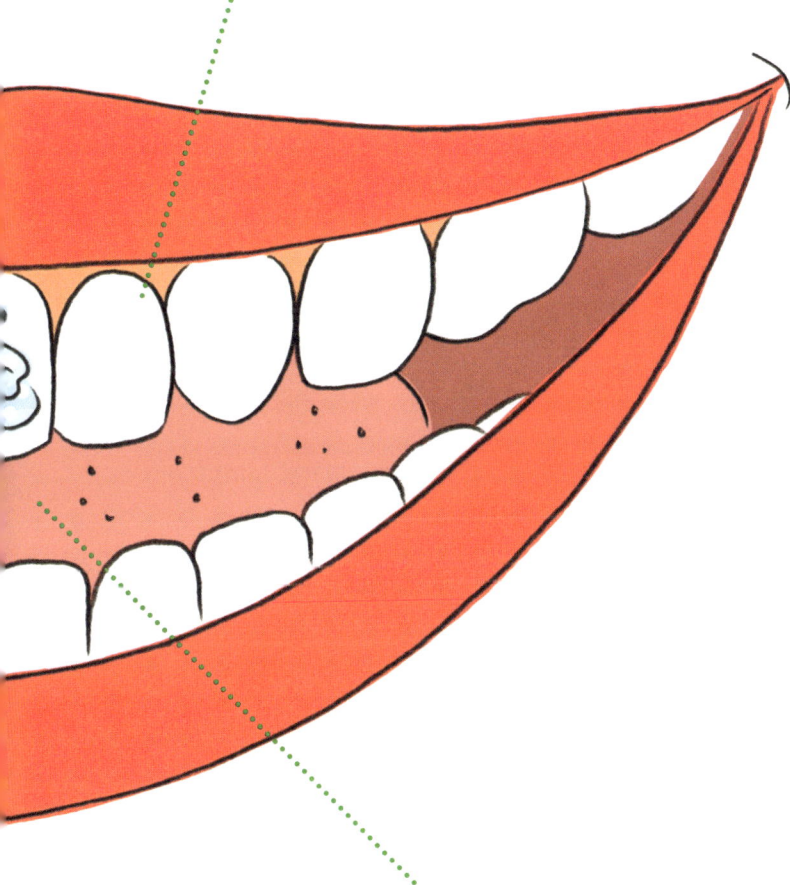

Tickle Your Tongue

Don't forget to brush your tongue, too! Freshly scrubbed taste buds are an important part of a clean mouth and fresh breath.

How to Brush

1. Hold your toothbrush at an angle to your gum line. Brush back and forth in small strokes, one tooth at a time. Repeat until you've scrubbed every single tooth.

2. Now do the inside of each tooth, using the same back-and-forth motion. Make sure to brush right up to the gum line.

3. Use the very tip of the brush to get behind your top and bottom front teeth.

How to Floss

1. Pull off a strand of floss about 18 inches long. Wind most of it around the middle finger of one hand, and the rest around the middle finger of the other.

2. Grip the floss between your thumbs and forefingers, stretching it tight. Push the floss gently between two of your teeth, wiggling it up and down the sides of both teeth and under the gum line. Imagine yourself scooping out little bits of food.

3. Unwind a little clean floss, winding up the used floss as you do so. Floss between two more teeth. Keep going, winding and flossing, until you've cleaned between all your teeth. Don't forget to floss at the very end of each row, behind your last tooth.

Healthy Gums

Think pink! Your gums need just as much attention as your teeth. If you don't take care of your gums, you could be setting yourself up for *gingivitis*—a disease that causes painful, red, swollen gums. To prevent gingivitis, floss once a day to fish out food lurking along the gum line. Dental floss comes in different thicknesses, waxed and unwaxed, to slide between your teeth comfortably. It even comes in tasty flavors!

Fresh Breath

Halitosis is a fancy way of saying "bad breath." But no matter what you call it, nothing shouts "Stand back!" quite as loudly. In rare cases mouth odor is caused by a nasal infection, upset stomach, or other problem that may need a doctor's attention. But it may just be a sign that you're skimping on brushing and flossing. Food between your teeth can rot and stink just like garbage. Clean it out!

Smile and Say "Calcium"!

For strong chompers, eat foods high in calcium, a mineral that helps toughen up teeth. You can find calcium in dairy products such as milk, cheese, and yogurt, as well as in non-dairy foods such as green leafy vegetables, black beans, and orange-colored fruits. A balanced, healthy diet that limits gooey, chewy, sticky snacks is the smartest choice.

Regular Visits

Does going to the dentist make your teeth chatter? You'll be less afraid if you know what to expect. Before the exam, ask your dentist to explain what will happen. And remember, regular checkups are the best way to avoid cavities and other problems that require special treatment.

Braces

Braces are a short-term investment in your long-term smile!

Grin and Bare 'Em

Today, millions of Americans—girls, grown-ups, even movie stars—are proudly sporting tin grins. If you're about to get braces, you may be nervous about what others will think or say. Perhaps you're braced for taunts of "Hey, metal mouth!" or "Woo-woo, train tracks!" You can rain on a bully's parade by taking the lead yourself. Give one and all a super-dazzling smile. If you *show* that you're confident, it will help you *feel* confident.

"Remember, you're not the only one in the world who has braces. Even adults wear them. Just smile. Braces are cool!"

Briana

Brushing

Brushing your teeth carefully is more important now than ever because food can get trapped on brackets and under wires. You should brush after every meal or snack. And at least once a day, devote several minutes to scouring all the nooks and crannies. If you don't, you may be in for a shock when your braces come off—an ugly line of tooth decay right where the braces used to be!

Flossing

With braces, it's especially important to floss your teeth daily. Most dentists say that bedtime is a good time, since you're more likely to slow down and do it right. Ask your orthodontist to show you how to thread the floss above your brackets. There's even a nifty tool that you can use.

A special brush called an *interproximal brush* scoots into the tight spots. Ask your orthodontist how to get one.

No-Go's

Hard foods can break your braces, and sticky foods will get, well, stuck in them. Cut apples and carrots into bite-size bits, and say "later" to caramels and gummy candy. For now, imagine the goodies you'll eat with your beautiful, straight teeth after the braces come off.

Rainbow Smile

Express your style every time you smile. You can choose bands for your brackets in all sorts of colors, from pastels to neon brights. Ask your orthodontist what choices are available to you.

Face

The skin on your face doesn't need a bunch of fancy lotions or potions—just a little tender loving care.

A Gentle Wash

Wash your face thoroughly at least once a day, especially at bedtime. Use a mild soap or facial cleanser—not a deodorant soap or a body bar meant to be used in the bath or shower. Use your hands or a soft, clean washcloth to gently wash your face. Use warm, not hot, water and rinse your skin well to remove all traces of soap.

Hands Off!

One of the best things you can do for your face is to keep your hands off it! Your fingers can spread oil and bacteria. When you do need to touch your face, use clean hands. And never pick at pimples—you could turn a tiny flare-up into a big-time breakout that leaves a scar.

Chapped Lips

If your lips are chapped, soothe them with a swoosh of lip balm. Look for one with sunscreen in it. Also, make sure you're drinking enough water. Dry, cracked lips may be your body's way of croaking "Help—I'm thirsty!"

The Skin You're In

The skin on your face is thinner and more sensitive than on other parts of your body, so be choosy about what you put on it. Look for unscented soaps and lotions that are labeled *hypoallergenic*, which means free of ingredients that can be irritating. If your skin is oily or prone to pimples, choose facial products that are oil-free or *non-comedogenic*—not likely to clog your pores. If your skin is dry, dab moisturizer or lotion only on the spots where it's needed.

Acne

Almost every girl comes face-to-face with skin flare-ups at some time. But you don't need to lose your head over them.

Acne Attack

Zits! Blackheads! Whiteheads! All of these bumps and blemishes are part of the package known as *acne*. Acne can appear for several reasons. During puberty, your body produces more oil, which combines with bacteria and dead skin cells to clog your pores—and that causes pimples. Family history also makes some people more likely to get acne. If you feel like pimples are picking on you, you're not alone. Almost every girl and boy in your school will have a battle with skin blemishes at one time or another.

Striking Back

While occasional bouts of acne are practically unavoidable, you may be able to prevent a few blemishes from becoming a full-blown breakout.

Keep your face clean. Wash your face daily with a mild soap or cleanser, but don't overdo it. Harsh scrubbing and rubbing can irritate already bothered skin.

Don't pick at or pop pimples. The oils and dirt on your fingers will only fan the flames of a flare-up. Plus, you can cause a permanent scar on your skin.

Check out the drugstore. Acne products can provide some relief for mild breakouts. Cruise the skin-care aisle at the drugstore, and read the labels carefully. Products that contain benzoyl peroxide help reduce oil and get rid of dead skin. But steer clear of products that contain alcohol—they can dry out your skin.

Talk to your doctor. Severe, out-of-control acne may call for medical attention. Your doctor can prescribe special creams or pills that are stronger than products available without a prescription.

A product with benzoyl peroxide may irritate sensitive skin. Before putting it on your face, test a little on the inside of your wrist to see if it gives you a rash. If it does, don't use it!

Sun Sense

On bright, sunny days and on snowy days, too, always bring your "sun sense" along with you.

Here's an easy way to remember how to protect your skin from the sun:

Slip on clothing that covers your skin from the sun's rays.

Slap on a hat with a broad brim that shades your face, ears, and neck.

Slop on sunscreen before venturing outdoors.

No Safe Tans

You may think a tan looks great now, but wrinkles and spots don't look good on anyone. Doctors agree: there's no such thing as a safe tan. All skin, regardless of type, is damaged by the sun. Exposing your unprotected skin can give you a blistering hot burn and eventually even lead to skin cancer.

Protect Your Skin

The sun's rays are most intense between ten o'clock in the morning and three o'clock in the afternoon, but dangerous rays are present all day long. Remember, too, that the sun can damage your skin even on cloudy days and in winter. The sun reflects off the clouds and snow, making it extra intense.

Before you head out the door, be sure to slather on some sunscreen. Sunscreen products carry a rating called an SPF, or sun protection factor. An SPF rating of 15 means that the sunscreen protects your skin 15 times longer than if you had used nothing at all. Everyone should use sunscreen with an SPF of at least 15. Girls with fair skin should use a product with an SPF of 30 or greater. Going swimming? Wear water-resistant sunscreen with an SPF of at least 45, no matter what color skin you have.

Reapply Often

If you're spending a lot of time outside, bring your sunscreen along and apply more every couple of hours. When you're at the beach or pool, it's especially important to put on more sunscreen after you get out of the water.

Beach Basics

Sandy beaches make the sun's rays even stronger. Take extra care by wearing lots of sunscreen and covering up with a hat and T-shirt. Of course, finding a shady spot to spend some time in is a good idea, too. Your skin will thank you!

Body Talk

Do you feel as if the whole world can spot every spot on your face? Keep your chin up. And give people something else to notice—your smile!

Freckle Face

I have freckles. I hate them and wish I could get some kind of lotion that would make my freckles go away. I need help!

freckles

There's no magic potion or lotion that will make your freckles disappear. But wearing a hat and plenty of sunscreen when you go out in the sun may keep you from getting more spots. And the next time you look in the mirror, practice pairing your freckles with a grin. See? Smiles and freckles are a winning combo! The fact is, most of us have something we'd like to change about ourselves. But try to think of your freckles as a special feature, something extra that makes you uniquely YOU.

Cold Sores

I have a big, ugly sore on my face right next to my mouth. My mom says it's a cold sore, but I don't even have a cold! This isn't the first time I've had this problem, either. How do I get rid of it?

Sore Spot

Cold sores, also called fever blisters, don't have anything to do with the common cold. They're caused by a virus similar to the one that causes chicken pox. While cold sores aren't serious, they can be an occasional nuisance. They often flare up when you're sick or stressed out, although there's no way to predict exactly when you'll get one. There are products you can buy at the drugstore to help get rid of the sores. If you have frequent, painful sores, your doctor may be able to prescribe stronger medication.

Bothersome Bangs

I just got bangs, but I've been having a problem with them. I've been getting pimples on my forehead. I've been washing my hair six times a week and putting medication on the pimples, but they still won't go away. Should I grow my bangs out?

Forehead Pimples

You are right to shampoo frequently. Girls who wear bangs need to keep their hair extra clean. Oils from your hair can irritate acne and make it worse. You'll also need to steer clear of hair products such as styling gels, sprays, and pomades that can leave a greasy film on your forehead. You don't have to banish bangs permanently, but you may need to pin them out of the way until your forehead clears up. Using headbands, barrettes, and other hair doo-dads is a fun and fashionable way to keep your bangs out of the zit zone. Ask the person who cuts your hair for some tips.

Zapped by Zits

I am 10 years old, and I have 13 zits. I've tried everything to get rid of them, but they always come back. I don't even eat a lot of junk food. Recently people have been calling me pizza face. What should I do?

Pizza Face

The sad truth is that you probably can't zap your zits completely. And though it's important to eat well, doctors agree that diet doesn't have much to do with acne. Talk to your doctor to see what else she recommends. Be patient. You may feel like you stand out now, but soon you won't be the only one under an acne attack. Pimples and puberty just seem to go together like pizza and pepperoni! The good news is that most acne clears up in the late teen years.

Reach!

Here's handy advice for grooming your **hands** so you can wave a happy hello. Plus everything you ever wanted to know about **underarms** and dealing with sweaty pits. And, finally, answers to all your questions about **breasts,** including hints for finding **bras** that really fit.

Hands

Keep your hands well groomed so you can put your best fingers forward for meeting and greeting people.

Clean Hands Win!

Keeping your hands clean is your first line of defense against picking up germs and bacteria. While alcohol-based hand sanitizers are widely available, washing your hands with soap and water is always the best choice—especially before you eat and always after you use the bathroom. If you have a cold, wash up often—especially after you blow your nose!

Battling Bad Habits

If you bite your nails or suck your thumb or fingers, you're not alone. The good news is that lots of girls have been able to break their bad habits with one of these tried-and-true tricks:

- Hold on to a small object, such as a stone or a ball, to keep your hands busy and out of your mouth.
- Coat your nails with a special bad-tasting polish, available at the drugstore.
- Wear gloves or mittens to bed so you can't suck your thumb or fingers in your sleep.
- Set up a reward system. Use a calendar to keep track of how many days you go without giving in to your habit, and give yourself a treat if you meet your goal.

If all else fails, talk to a doctor or dentist for ideas. But don't give up—it takes time and patience to undo habits you've had for years.

Warts

Warts are harmless little bumps of flesh, usually white or pinkish in color. They're caused by viruses passed from one person to another. Warts often go away by themselves but can take a long time—up to a year or two! To speed up the process, ask a parent for help using a wart-removing product (from a drugstore). Or try this: put a piece of duct tape over the wart and leave it on for five or six days. Then remove it for a day to let the skin air out. Put a new piece on for another five or six days. After a few rounds of this, your wart should be gone. If your warts are really annoying you, ask your doctor to remove them using a special freezing process.

Calluses

Calluses are hard, rough patches of skin caused by friction. Your body grows a layer of tough skin to protect the area. Athletes such as gymnasts get a lot of calluses, but you can get them just from raking leaves or gripping the handlebars of your bike. Wear gloves to help prevent calluses.

Nail Care

Scraggly, dirty fingernails are a sorry sight. Scrub your nails with a soft-bristled nail brush to remove the dirt trapped underneath.

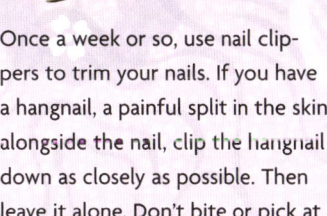

Once a week or so, use nail clippers to trim your nails. If you have a hangnail, a painful split in the skin alongside the nail, clip the hangnail down as closely as possible. Then leave it alone. Don't bite or pick at it. That will make it worse.

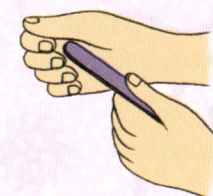

Use an emery board to round off any sharp corners or ragged edges.

Underarms

In the past you probably never gave your armpits a second thought. But now that you're growing up, it's time to start paying attention to them.

Antiperspirants help prevent pit stains. Your clothes—and your friends—will thank you!

B.O.—It's the Pits!

Sweating is natural and healthy. It's your body's way of cooling down. But you may be sweating more than ever before and in different places, such as under your arms. And when the sweat mixes with bacteria on your skin and meets the air, it can smell! Luckily, keeping body odor in check isn't hard. You can start by giving your armpits a good sudsing every time you shower or bathe.

Deodorants and Antiperspirants

Once you've washed your armpits, you may want to use an underarm product that helps keep the sweat, odor, or both away. *Deodorants* work to prevent underarm odor. *Antiperspirants* actually work to reduce sweating. Some products are both an antiperspirant and a deodorant. They come in roll-ons, solid sticks, gels, and sprays—pick the one that works best for you.

Underarm Hair

If you haven't already sprouted hair under your arms, you will soon. Some girls don't like it. Others aren't bothered by it one little bit. Whether you want to remove it or leave it there is a very personal decision. If you feel you'd be more comfortable without underarm hair, ask your mom if you can remove it. Shaving is the most common way to get rid of underarm hair. While shaving may seem scary at first, it quickly becomes second nature. Ask your mom or older sister for a lesson.

Breasts

Budding breasts are one of the first signs that you're entering puberty and that your body is starting to take on a new shape.

Time to Grow

You'll probably start to notice changes in your breasts between the ages of 9 and 12, although some girls start earlier or later. There's no way to predict how big your breasts will get—you won't necessarily take after your mother or older sister. And don't worry if you notice one breast growing more quickly than the other. The two will eventually even out, although they'll never be exactly alike.

Stages of Development

Doctors divide breast development into the five stages shown below. See if you can tell what stage you're in, and sneak a peek at what's coming next.

If you don't seem to go through every stage, don't panic. Some girls may skip over one of the middle stages.

Stage 1

This is how most breasts look before puberty begins. Breasts are flat to the chest, with a raised nipple and small areola.

Stage 2

A raised bump called a breast bud begins to develop under each nipple. The nipples and areolas get larger and darker. You may feel some tenderness in this area as the breasts grow.

How Long Does It Take?

There's no way to know how long each stage will last or how long it will take for your breasts to become fully developed. Most girls reach stage 5 about four to five years after their breasts begin developing, or around age 17 or 18.

Shapes, Sizes, and Colors

Breasts come in endless varieties. Some are big, some are small. Some are round, some are more pointy. Some sit high on the chest, some hang low. Some point up, some point down. Even the colors of the nipples and *areolas,* the dark circular areas around the nipples, vary from pink to dark brown. Some nipples stick out, while others are *inverted,* or go inward. Some girls may discover small hairs growing around their areolas. This is normal. Don't pick at or try to pluck out the hairs. Doing so can irritate the sensitive skin in this area and cause an infection.

Stage 3
The nipple and areola continue to grow and can get even darker in color. Breasts get larger and may look a bit pointy.

Stage 4
The areola and nipple blend together into a mound that rises above the breast. Some girls skip this stage.

Stage 5
Breasts are fully developed, with a rounder, fuller shape. The areola and nipple form a mound that rises above the breast. The nipple is raised above it.

Bras

Do You Need a Bra?

There's no right answer to this question. There's only what's right for you. Do you feel self-conscious because your growing breasts show through your shirt? Are you uncomfortable when you play sports? Generally, you need a bra when you feel that you'd be more comfortable with one than without one.

"Girls should wear bras to be comfortable. It's up to the girl herself to decide when the time is right." *Katelyn*

First Things First

If you've decided it's time to get a bra, you'll need to talk with your mom or another adult family member before you head for the mall. Work up your courage and state your case as clearly as possible. Tell your mom or family member that you feel you're ready for a bra. Explain why you think you need one, and ask if she'll take you shopping for one. If she doesn't agree that you need one, offer to compromise by starting with a sports bra or training bra. They're described on pages 48–49.

No One Has to Know

What if you're ready to wear a bra but you're not ready for the whole world to know? Don't worry. Bras come in plenty of neutral colors that will match your skin tone. You don't have to buy the bras with bright colors or eye-popping prints that will show through your shirts.

Do you feel left out because everyone except you is getting a bra? Try a tank top or camisole under your shirt—no one will be able to tell if you're wearing a bra or not.

Sizing Up Sizes

Once you've decided to buy a bra, you'll need to figure out what size you wear. Bra sizes have two parts: a number and a letter. The number relates to the size of your rib cage. The letter—or cup size—relates to the size of your breasts. But don't worry too much about figuring out your exact bra size. It's only meant as a starting point. Every bra is different, and you may have to try on several different ones to find the right fit for you.

Adjusting the Fit

Once you've found the right size, you may still need to make some adjustments. Depending on the style of your bra, you may be able to tighten or loosen the fit around your rib cage by moving the hook over one or two notches. You may also be able to make the shoulder straps longer or shorter. To see if the straps are the right length, wiggle your shoulders. If the straps slide off, shorten them. If they feel as though they're biting into your skin, let them out a bit.

There's no reason to wear a bra while you sleep. It won't affect your shape or size. Put your bra on in the morning and take it off at night.

Find Your Size

1. Measure around your ribs below your breasts to get your rib size. Look on the chart to find the number for that size.

Rib size	=	Rib number
22–23 inches		28
24–25 inches		30
26–27 inches		32
28–29 inches		34
30–31 inches		36

2. Measure around your chest over your nipples to get your chest size. Subtract the rib number you got above from this size. Look on the chart to find your cup letter.

Chest size—

Rib number	=	Cup letter
–1		AAA
0		AA
1		A
2		B
3		C
4		D

3. Your bra size is your rib number and cup letter. An example: 32A.

Bra Browsing

Bras come in oodles of styles, fabrics, and colors. You'll need to try on lots to find a good fit, so look for a store with a large selection. Ask your mom, your older sister, or an adult friend to go with you. They can help adjust straps and fetch more sizes for you. When you find a bra that looks smooth under your shirt and doesn't pinch, scratch, or ride up your back, buy it!

Training Bras

A bra with an A to AAA cup is often called a training bra. This bra doesn't train your breasts to do anything—it trains you to get used to wearing a bra! Even if you don't need it for support, wearing one may make you feel less self-conscious and more confident about how you look.

Built-In Bras

Many tank tops come with an extra piece of material called a "built-in" or "shelf" bra. Because the bra is attached to the tank, most girls don't need to wear anything else supportive underneath. You might have noticed these bras in clothing well before you ever needed a bra— that's OK! There's no harm in having it in there.

Soft-Cup Bras

You guessed it—soft-cup bras are soft and flexible. For most girls who wear a size B cup or smaller, the elastic band in a soft-cup bra provides all the support they need, plus a comfortable fit.

Sports Bras

A sports bra looks like a cut-off tank top with a wide elastic band at the bottom. It's designed to hold your breasts snugly against your chest so that they don't bounce around while you're running or jumping. You can wear a sports bra every day if you like how it looks and feels.

Body Talk

Too big? Too small? No matter how they're built, many girls feel their breasts just aren't right. And that's just plain wrong!

Body Bullies

Some of the boys in my class make fun of me because my chest is practically flat! They are always making up poems and songs about me.

Tired of Boys

Rude remarks can really smart! What you need to do is remember to look at the big picture. Are your breasts really the most important part of you? No way! What about your straight A's in math, your perfect back flip, or your kindness to family and friends? That's the real you, the girl inside who really matters. Don't lose sight of her for a second, even when others seem to. If the teasing gets worse, or if a boy's words or actions make you feel threatened or afraid, tell a parent or teacher immediately. Nobody has the right to harass you or to make you feel unsafe.

Pump Up the Pasta?

I don't have any breasts! I was wondering if there were any foods to give me the nutrients to grow breasts.

flat Chest

Lots of girls wish there were a miracle diet or magic exercise that would make their breasts blossom overnight. But no food you eat will make a beeline to your breasts. And all the push-ups in the world won't increase your cup size. Breasts are made mostly of fatty tissue and milk ducts, so there are no muscles in them to flex. Beware of advertisements for diets, drugs, or fancy gadgets that claim to boost your bust. Their claims are just flat-out lies.

Too Busty

I have bigger boobs than all of my friends. Because of this, my friends are embarrassed to be around me because they think I'm very ugly and fat. I used to be very popular, but now I find myself dorky and lonely.

Desperate For Help

You're not dorky—you're developing. And though you wish otherwise, your body has a schedule all its own. For every girl like you who's sad because her breasts are growing quickly, there's another girl who's upset that hers are still flat. And it's just plain wrong to be mean to someone because her body is changing. Choose outfits that make you feel comfortable and confident. Make sure your bra fits properly. You might even try wearing sports bras. Their extra-snug support may lift your spirits, too. No matter what you wear, stand up straight and proud. If you feel good about yourself, you'll be less of a target for teasers.

Faking It

I am really flat-chested. All the girls have big breasts except me. Should I stuff? I'm worried the tissue might fall out when I'm running.

Stuff?

Who wants wads of itchy tissue stuffed down her shirtfront? You don't need that sort of trickery. Chances are you won't fool anyone, but you might feel like a fool when some eagle eye calls your bluff. It's hard not to compare yourself to other girls or to the images you see on TV and in magazines, but never forget that it's the stuff in your head and heart—not the stuff in your sweater—that determines how you really measure up.

Belly Zone

This section is all about your midsection! Tall, short, straight, curvy—find out why all girls should celebrate their unique **shapes and sizes.** Learn how to **eat well** and be choosy about the **food** you chew.

Shapes & Sizes

All Different Shapes

The shape of your body—your basic frame—is something you're born with, like the shape of your nose or the color of your eyes. Some girls are tall and lanky, while others are short and sturdy. Some girls are curvy, while others are more straight. Usually your body shape resembles the shape of others in your family. No one body type is better or worse than another. All can be fit, healthy, and beautiful.

"Your weight depends on how your body is built. Also, your body hasn't finished developing yet. Just remember, you were made beautifully. Don't listen to anyone who says you're not!"

Sam

Beware of fad diets and fancy weight-loss programs you see advertised online and in magazines. Always ask your doctor about a diet before you try it!

All Different Sizes

Many girls worry about whether their weight is "normal" for their age. But there's no such thing as one ideal weight, especially during puberty, when girls' bodies are growing quickly and changing shape. There's a wide range of weights that doctors consider normal for any girl, depending on her height and basic body type. If you're concerned about your weight, don't decide on your own to go on a diet. Talk to your doctor first to find out if it's necessary. Together you can set weight and fitness goals based on what's healthiest for you and what makes sense for your particular body type.

Where's My Waist?

As your body changes and your weight begins to shift, you may go through a period when your waist "thickens," or gets bigger. It doesn't mean you're getting fat. It means you're filling out. Your waistline will reappear as your body develops.

Food

Fuel up! Healthy eating habits give your body the extra energy it needs to grow during puberty.

Eating a Balanced Diet

While there are certainly foods that are good for your body and foods that are not, this doesn't mean that you cannot enjoy your treats. Some foods—such as whole grains, lean proteins, fruits, and vegetables—have more nutrients than others. They make you feel more energetic by providing healthy fuel, so these are the foods that you should eat most of the time. Other foods are higher in fat or sugar, but they are OK occasionally—you don't have to deny yourself completely. Part of the fun of a campfire is s'mores, and there's nothing like cold ice cream on a hot summer day. The key is moderation. That means not eating too much (or sometimes too little) of anything. Make sure your meals and snacks are a mix of many different kinds of foods. No girl can live on candy bars or carrot sticks alone.

Knowing When to Eat

Do you eat when you're bored? Do treats and TV go together? Do you reach into the fridge out of habit, whether you're hungry or not? You may be eating when you don't need to. How do you know when to eat? Listen to your body. Try to eat only when you're hungry, and stop when you're full. Eat a snack if you think you need an energy boost. But don't eat just because you're nervous, bored, or craving a favorite flavor. Eating should be a pleasure, not a pastime.

Smart Snacks

For most girls, three square meals aren't enough to get through a busy day. Mini meals of fruit, raw veggies, cheese, low-fat yogurt, or whole-grain crackers spread with nut butter can fill in the gaps. When you're packing your lunch, include a healthful snack to munch on between school and soccer or ballet and babysitting.

Best Beverages

Water is the best beverage around, and your body thirsts for it. Make sure you drink plenty of it every day, especially during and after exercise. Soda pop and punch—even fruit juices—are high in sugar and should be viewed as "seldom snacks." Milk (fat-free or low-fat) is always a healthier choice.

Going Vegetarian

Thousands of girls and their families have chosen to eliminate meat and other animal products from their diets. Some do it because of their beliefs. Others do it for health reasons. A vegetarian diet can easily supply all the nutrients you need. But if you're thinking about becoming a vegetarian, first do some homework. It isn't simply a matter of passing over the hamburger and filling up on fries. You'll need to learn what foods to eat to get enough protein, vitamins, and minerals.

Nutrition

Pack your meals and snacks with healthy foods.

A Balancing Act

Eating right can be easy to do when you understand which foods are good for you and how much of those foods you should be eating. To help, the United States Department of Agriculture (USDA) has created MyPlate, showing the types of foods—particularly fruits, vegetables, grains, proteins, and dairy products—that you should be eating at each meal. As a general rule, about half your plate should contain fruits and veggies. According to the USDA, a girl who is ten years old and gets a minimum of 60 minutes of moderate to vigorous exercise a day should aim to eat the following:

Grains, such as
- whole wheat
- popcorn
- oats
- brown rice
- wild rice

Fruits, such as
- bananas
- oranges
- raisins
- apples
- peaches
- pears

Fruits

Grains

Dairy

Veggies

Protein

Dairy products, such as
- milk
- yogurt
- cheese
- calcium-fortified soy milk

Vegetables, such as
- spinach
- tomatoes
- avocado
- cucumbers
- green peas
- acorn squash

Proteins, such as
- chicken or turkey
- beef
- almonds, peanuts, and other nuts and nut butters
- salmon, tuna, and other fish
- tofu
- eggs

Enjoy food, but don't stuff yourself!

If you've ever eaten too much candy at Halloween or loaded up at a meal such as Thanksgiving dinner, you know how it feels to have eaten too much at one time. The MyPlate diagram should help you better understand what foods you should eat, but here are some extra tips that might help you choose to consume the right amount:

- Use a smaller plate, bowl, or glass. You'll be more aware of portion size.
- Avoid ordering value-size meals at restaurants.
- Stop eating when you are no longer hungry, not when you are full.
- Slow down while you eat. Food need time to digest, so it takes a while to satisfy your hunger.
- When eating out, share too-big portions or set aside the extra food to bring home and eat later.
- Write down what you eat. You might be surprised to see how much—or how little—you're really taking in. Adjust your portion sizes as needed. Get help from your mom or dad if you're unsure.

Be a Savvy Snacker

Instead of . . .

Choose . . .

french fries,

popcorn sprinkled with
Parmesan cheese.

a bowl of ice cream,

low-fat frozen yogurt.

a bag of chips,

a handful of roasted almonds.

a milk shake,

a fresh-fruit smoothie.

Tips

- Eat a rainbow of colorful veggies, from green kale to orange squash!
- Choose fruits for desserts instead of sugary treats.
- Skip sugary drinks and drink water instead. There are nearly 10 packets of sugar per can of soda.
- Rely on fat-free or low-fat (1%) milk, yogurt, cheese, and other dairy products.
- Go easy on processed meats such as hot dogs, pepperoni, and sausage.

Less Is Best

Beyond the basic food groups, there are also "empty calories," which are extras such as the oils, fats, sugars, and salt that are in many of the foods you eat. These should be eaten sparingly. A little butter or sweetener goes a long way.

Your Personal Plate

Every girl's dietary needs are different. To find out what balanced diet is perfect for you, ask a parent, teacher, or librarian to help you look online at **www.ChooseMyPlate.gov.**

What makes a girl glow from head to toe? A daily diet rich in all the essential vitamins and minerals!

Vitamin A
For sparkling eyes, sharp night vision, and smooth skin: eat apricots, nectarines, carrots, spinach, sweet potatoes, and squash.

The B Vitamins
For healthy red blood cells and plenty of energy: eat meat, fish, poultry, whole-grain products, leafy green vegetables, and dried beans.

Vitamin C
For strong teeth, gums, and bones, and to ward off colds: eat oranges, strawberries, broccoli, peppers, spinach, and kiwi.

Vitamin D
For strong teeth and bones: drink lots of milk and eat eggs, salmon, and liver.

Vitamin E
To protect the tissue in your skin, eyes, liver, and lungs: eat sunflower seeds, leafy green vegetables, nuts, and avocados.

Vitamin K

For blood that clots quickly when you're cut: eat kale, spinach, Brussels sprouts, and other dark greens.

Iron

For a healthy blood supply that's full of oxygen: eat red meat, baked potatoes, apricots, raisins, beans, iron-fortified whole grain breads, and dark leafy greens.

Calcium

For straight, tall posture and a great grin: eat yogurt, cheese, and broccoli. Drink three to four glasses of milk a day.

Body Talk

Weight worries and food fears can make some girls miserable at mealtime.

Fat or Thin?

People say I'm thin, but I think I need to lose about 15 pounds. I'm 11 years old and weigh a whopping 90 pounds. Don't I need to lose some weight?

Too Fat

Ask your doctor. If she says your weight is fine, then it is! But your thinking may need some shaping up. When some girls see super-skinny people in ads and on TV, they get tricked into worrying about their own bodies. They see themselves as fat when they're not. This can be unhealthy if it causes a girl to try to lose weight when she shouldn't. If you don't believe people when they say you're slim, talk with your parent, doctor, or school counselor. They can help you see yourself just as you are—and teach you to like what you see.

Friend vs. Others

My friend is always comparing herself to other girls. She's always saying that she's jealous of how thin and developed I am. It makes me sad that she thinks she's not good enough. But my friend isn't the only one who does this—lots of my friends do. Why?

Confused

Most girls compare themselves to other girls—especially during puberty, when everyone is changing at different times, in different ways. You might find yourself checking out everyone else to see where you fit in. That's normal. But here's the thing: When you compare yourself to others, it's easy to find things about your body that you don't like. And that can make you feel bad. It might be hard, but girls have to learn to love how they're made and try to stop the comparing. Next time your friend talks about being unhappy with her body, just say, "You're great the way you are" or "I know how you feel. I don't like some things about myself too, but I focus on the things I DO like."

Junk-Food Junkie

I have a problem with eating junk food.
I am thin now, but soon all this eating
will catch up to me and my weight.
Plus, junk food is not good for your
complexion. How can I get off my urge
to eat and eat and EAT junk food?

WORRIED

Eating junk food every now and then is
not necessarily a health disaster. And doctors no longer believe that it causes skin
woes. The problem with junk food is that
it simply doesn't have much nutritional
value—it fills you up without giving you
the nutrients you need. There's no quick
fix to nix your junk-food cravings. Try
cutting back gradually by substituting
healthier snacks, such as fruit instead of
cookies, or frozen yogurt instead of ice
cream. Don't expect to cut junk food out
of your life entirely. It's easier to allow
yourself an occasional treat than to stick
to a strict, junk-food-free diet.

Mirror, Mirror

I think I look fat. I know I'm not, but
I just can't help feeling this way and hating
the way I look. I'm miserable. Some days
I don't even want to be seen. I exercise,
but I still feel too big. What do I do?

Big Thinker

Your body might be growing and changing
exactly as it should be, but when you look
at your reflection, it sounds as if you see
something else. Sometimes your brain can
play tricks on your eyes. Many girls—and
women, too—have experienced seeing
themselves as bigger or smaller than they
actually are. It's important to see your
body as it really is, so talk to a parent
about this. If you need to lose some
weight, that's one thing. But if your brain is
just seeing your body in a way that's not
true, you might need help changing that.
It's the kind of thing that sometimes can
crush your self-esteem or steer you
toward an eating disorder. Try not to
obsess over the mirror until you and your
parent figure this out.

Big Changes

Whether you've already sprouted **new hair** and started your **period,** or whether you're still waiting for these big changes to happen, this section answers all the important questions, from using **pads** to the truth about **PMS.** Armed with the facts, you'll be able to relax.

Pubic Area

The area below your belly button will undergo some pretty big changes during puberty.

It's normal for pubic hair to appear over a period of years, so don't be surprised if this process seems as slow as watching grass grow.

Pubic Hair

As your body begins to change and develop, you will notice new hair in places that were once pretty smooth. The pubic area is the triangular patch between your hip bones and thighs. When hair grows here, it's called *pubic hair*. At first, the hair looks straight, kind of like the hair on your arms or legs. For many girls, it is dark—almost black—but for others it matches the color of the hair on their heads. There are girls who have small patches of straight hair in their pubic areas from the time they are babies, and there are others who notice it only when their bodies start to develop. Pubic hair takes a long time to appear. It eventually changes from fine, straight hair to coarse, curly hair.

Other Changes

You may notice a sticky liquid in your underpants. This is called *vaginal discharge,* and it is totally normal. It is coming from your vagina, is usually clear or whitish, and has very little smell. Your vagina makes the discharge to keep itself clean. Some days you might have none at all; other days you might notice it a couple of times.

If the discharge has a different color or a strong smell, this can be the sign of an infection. It can look greenish or white, and your vaginal area may even feel itchy or swollen. If any of these things is happening, talk to your parents and see your doctor.

Strip Clean

Take off damp or sweaty clothes as soon as possible. Bathing suits, tights, and leotards made of nylon and other synthetic fabrics can cause rashes and infections. Be sure to wash these garments frequently.

Get into Cotton

Whether you wear bikinis or briefs, buy underpants that are made of all cotton or have a cotton lining. Cotton breathes, or lets moisture pass through and evaporate. That means less risk of irritation and infection.

Fresh Start

Put on a clean pair of underpants at the start of every day and after every shower or bath. It's the simplest way to stay fresh.

Period

Getting your period. There are probably no other words that will make you feel as excited, scared, or just plain confused.

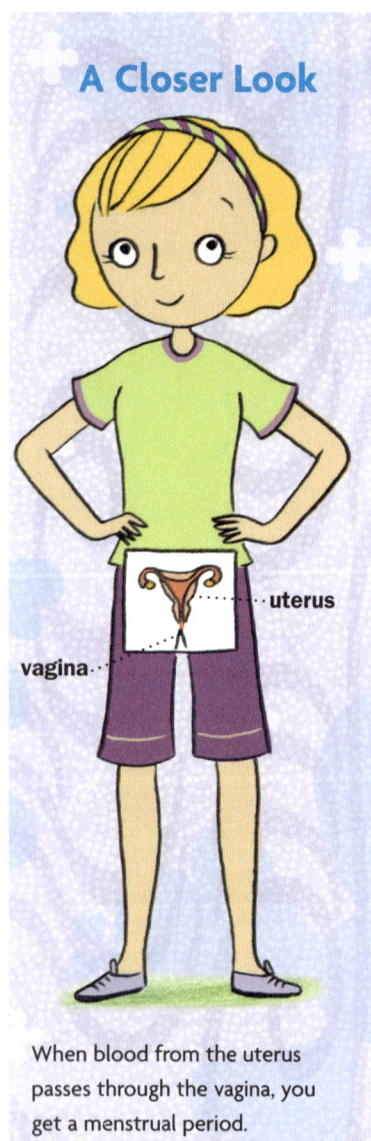

A Closer Look

uterus

vagina

When blood from the uterus passes through the vagina, you get a menstrual period.

The Basic Facts

So what's a period, anyway? It's short for *menstrual period*—the time each month when fluid containing blood flows out of the *uterus* through the vagina. The amount is small, about 3 tablespoons. This flow usually lasts two to eight days. Some girls have a menstrual period every 25 days. Other girls get them up to 40 days apart. All are normal. When you first start getting your period, though, the length of time between periods —and the number of days the blood flow lasts— may change each month. After a while your periods will get more regular.

At first, the idea of getting periods may seem, well— gross. But periods are a sign that your body is healthy and working properly. It's preparing to do the grown-up work of having a baby someday. Every month your body practices for this by building a "nest," a place for a baby to grow inside your uterus. The nest is a lining of blood and other fluid that builds up on the uterus walls. Because there's no baby, the lining is shed and you have a period. It's all controlled by hormones, the chemicals that change your body from little girl to grown-up woman.

Telltale Signs

Most girls start to get periods between the ages of 9 and 15. You can't predict exactly when you'll get your first period, but your body may give you clues that it's on its way. Most girls start to menstruate, or get periods, a couple years after their breasts have started developing and their pubic hair has begun growing in. Can other people tell whether you've gotten your period yet? Nope! Not unless you tell them.

Your First Time

So the day comes when you get your period. It may announce itself with a bright red, rusty red, or dark brown stain in your underpants. What do you do? Don't panic. Wipe yourself as well as you can. If you haven't got a pad or tampon—or you don't know how to use one—fold up a wad of toilet paper, tissues, or paper towels to put into your underwear.

Find your mom, an older sister, or a woman you trust. Take a deep breath and say, "I think I just got my period. Do you have something I can use?" You may feel like crawling into a hole, but remember, getting your period is normal. There's no reason to be ashamed. The older person will probably remember how it felt her first time and will be glad to help.

Keep a supply of pads or tampons on hand so you're always prepared. Once you know you won't be taken by surprise, you can R-E-L-A-X.

If your period catches you by surprise at school, ask a teacher or school nurse for help.

Buying Supplies

Deciding which "feminine hygiene" products to use can seem overwhelming at first, but your choices are actually pretty simple: pads or tampons. Pads are specially designed tissues that fit into the crotch of your underpants. They are made of layers of absorbent material that collect blood as it leaves your body, and they stick to your underwear with double-sided tape. Tampons are also specially designed tissues, but these are inserted into the vagina and absorb the blood before it leaves your body. Both tampons and pads come in a variety of shapes and sizes, and the one you use will depend upon your activities and whether your blood flow is light or heavy. When girls first get their period, most start with pads—in fact,

Pads

Pads are convenient and easy to use. Almost all pads have a sticky strip on the back that attaches to your underpants. Others have wide "wings" that wrap around the edges of your underpants for added coverage.

Panty Liners

Panty liners, or panty shields, are very thin pads. They're best for days when your flow is light, or when you suspect your period might start and you want to be prepared. Some girls like to wear a panty liner along with a tampon in case the tampon leaks.

many girls don't try tampons until they are older. You can talk to your mom to figure out what works best for you.

Scented vs. Unscented

Most pads and tampons are available in both deodorant and nondeodorant versions. Deodorant products have perfumes and other chemicals to fight odor caused by fluids and moisture trapped in the pad or tampon. But they can also irritate skin and cause allergic reactions. You're better off using unscented products and keeping yourself fresh by changing your pads and tampons regularly.

Tampons

Tampons are good for sports, especially swimming, because they're worn inside the body. The vagina muscles hold the tampon in place so it can't slip out. A string hangs outside your body so you can pull the tampon out.

When to Change

It's a good idea to replace your pad or tampon every two to four hours to prevent leaks and odor. If you have to go to the bathroom in the meantime, you can hold the string of the tampon out of the way so it doesn't get wet. Never leave a tampon in place for more than six to eight hours—you could get a serious infection called toxic shock syndrome. At night, use a pad. Change pads right before you go to bed and again first thing in the morning.

What to Do with the Used One

Whether you're at home or away, be sure to dispose of your used pads, tampons, applicators, and outer wrappings appropriately. This means wrapping pads in toilet paper and placing them in the nearest wastebasket. Some public restrooms have a bin in each stall for this purpose. Never flush a pad or tampon down the toilet. Some tampon applicators are flushable. Check to see if the box says "flushable applicators." If not, wrap the applicator in toilet paper and throw it out.

Is It Over Yet?

Once your periods become regular, which usually happens within one to two years, they should last about the same length of time each month. You'll be able to tell when your period is winding down because the flow is usually heaviest in the beginning or middle and then starts to trickle off toward the end. You may not see any blood on the pad or in the tampon for several hours or even a whole day. The color may change, too—from bright red to brown. It's a good idea to wear a panty liner for a day or two even after you think your period is over. If you go more than two days without seeing any blood, your period is probably finished.

Wrappers from tampons and pads go in the wastebasket—not down the toilet.

Keeping Track

At first, it can be tricky to predict when your periods will arrive. Use a calendar to keep track of when they start and end. After a while, your cycle should become regular enough for you to be able to figure out when to expect your period.

Tampons

Most girls use pads when they first get their period. But eventually, some girls switch over to tampons. There is no rush to do this—it's a very personal choice and one that you will want to discuss with your mom.

When girls first start using tampons, they generally pick the smallest ones. These are called "junior," "slim," or "slender." These tampons are skinnier and smaller than most others, so they are easier for girls to use.

Most tampons come with an applicator, which is a pair of tubes that help to insert the tampon. Some girls find that plastic applicators (compared to cardboard applicators) are easier to use at first. The applicator does not stay inside your body. Once the tampon has been inserted, the applicator comes out and should be thrown away in the trash. There is more information about tampons in *The Care and Keeping of You 2* and in the instructional information provided inside tampon boxes.

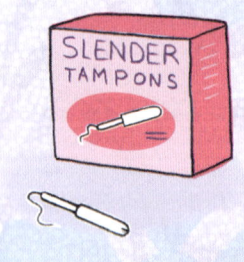

How to Use a Pad

Pads are a great way to get started when you first get your period. But while they're simple to use, they do take some getting used to. Follow the steps below to help you through your first time.

1. Get Ready

You can put a pad in your underpants anytime you want. Some girls like to wear thin pads every day because of vaginal discharge, and that's fine. When you have your period, though, you may want to use thicker pads because they absorb better.

2. Unpeel

If your pad comes individually wrapped, remove the packaging. Remove the paper covering the tape on the back of the pad and lay the pad inside your underpants so that it fits along the crotch. If your pad has wings, fold those around the edges of your underpants after you have placed the pad.

3. Check Fit

When you pull up your underpants, the pad may feel a little bulky—that's OK. It shouldn't irritate your thighs or prevent your underpants from being pulled all the way up. Make sure your pad sits in the middle of the crotch of your underpants—not too far forward or too far back.

4. Removal

Most girls change their pads each time they go to the bathroom. If your flow is heavy, you may want to change it more frequently. Remove the pad by peeling it off of your underpants from one end; then roll the pad onto itself from one end to the other. You can wrap the rolled pad in a piece of tissue or toilet paper and throw it away in the trash. Wash your hands.

Pad Pointers

There are so many different shapes and sizes of pads available. How do you know which ones to use?

Panty liners are super-thin pads. Most girls use them at the very end of their period when there is only a little bit of bleeding. Some girls even use them when they don't have their period because they don't like the feeling of vaginal discharge.

Regular pads may look thin, but they are very absorbent. These pads are usually longer than panty liners and hold more blood. They can be used anytime during your period, though if your flow is heavy you will need to change your pad more often.

Maxi pads used to be really big—almost an inch thick! Now they look almost as thin as a regular pad, but they are much more absorbent. Maxi pads are great for heavy flow days.

Pads with wings are pads (panty liner, regular, or maxi) that have extra material on the sides. This material helps absorb blood that might spill a little bit over the edge of a pad. This helps keep your underpants nice and clean. When you use a pad with wings, tape the main part of the pad down first and the wings second. When you remove the pad, lift up the wings first and the main part second.

What Is PMS?

Once you begin to menstruate regularly, you may notice some patterns in how you feel right before your period. Sometimes these physical and emotional changes are referred to as *premenstrual syndrome,* or PMS for short. It's not a disease or an illness, just a natural part of your menstrual cycle. PMS is caused by hormones—chemicals that are released in your body at this time. The symptoms you feel can be a clue to when your period is coming, so you'll want to pay attention to them.

Physical Signs

A week or two before your period, your breasts may feel swollen or more tender than usual. You may also notice that your body feels heavier, even puffy, and that your skin is more prone to breakouts. All of these symptoms will go away after your period begins. You may also feel cramps in your lower abdomen or back before and during your period. The cramps happen because the muscles of the uterus are hard at work.

Emotional Signs

Your periods can also affect your moods. Some girls feel tired, irritated, grouchy—more emotional—in the days leading up to their periods. If you find that your feelings are more intense during this time, know that this is perfectly normal. But when you're feeling extra edgy, try not to unleash your frustration on family and friends. Instead, try talking to them about how you feel. Doing so may bring kind words of support just when you need them most. And don't forget to treat yourself to some quiet time alone. Listen to music, take a walk, or write in a journal. You'll be glad you did!

Your feelings are important, so pay attention to them. Don't let anyone tell you they're stupid or silly, or that they don't matter.

How to Feel Better

The best remedies for premenstrual aches and pains are fairly simple: eat right, exercise, give yourself a break when needed, and treat yourself to some soothing heat.

Ahhh—Heat!

A warm bath or a hot-water bottle laid over your tummy can help soothe cramps.

Medications

If headaches, backaches, or cramps make you feel crummy, there is medication at the drugstore that you can try. Talk to your mom or doctor to see what she recommends.

Healthy Eating

Cut down on salty foods such as pretzels and chips before your period. Salt makes your body retain water, giving you that puffy, bloated feeling. Eat plenty of fruits and veggies instead.

Exercise

Stay active! Exercise is a great way to ease aches and pains and to lift your spirits, too. A brisk walk, a few laps in the pool, or a bike ride in the fresh air is always good medicine.

Body Talk

If you feel like your menstrual cycle is taking you for a ride, don't worry. In no time at all, you'll learn to take your periods in stride.

Sneak Attacks

What if my period starts in school or in church or in a public place and I don't have a pad or tampon? And what if it leaks on my clothes before I can stop it?

Scared

If you get caught unprepared, don't panic. Make a temporary pad out of folded toilet paper, facial tissue, or paper towel to put in your underpants. Then ask the school nurse, a teacher, or a friend if she has a spare pad or tampon. Some public restrooms have coin-operated machines where you can buy pads and tampons. If you do leak, tie a sweater, shirt, or jacket around your waist to make a fashionable cover-up until you can change clothes. Chances are, nobody will notice a thing! P.S. Cold water is best for getting blood stains out of clothes.

Tampons vs. Pads

How am I supposed to know if a pad or tampon is right for me?

Just wondering

It all depends on what you're most comfortable with. Both are safe and reliable if used properly, so you really can't go wrong either way. Some girls who play sports prefer tampons because they don't show through a uniform or bathing suit, and they can be worn in water. Some girls like tampons because they keep you feeling dry—you can hardly tell you have your period! But other girls like pads because they're so simple to use. They're easy to change, and easy to know when to change. Don't be afraid to experiment with tampons and pads to figure out which you like best.

Miserable, Period.

I've had my period for a year now, and I still haven't gotten used to walking around feeling like I've wet my pants. I'm the only one of my girlfriends who has it. My mom is here to talk to me about it, but I don't want to. I don't want to keep it to myself, either. I feel like I don't even want to grow up!

I don't want to grow up!

You sound lonely, scared, and uncomfortable, and that's a heavy load for any girl to bear. For starters, it might help to change your pad more often or consider giving tampons a try. Both will make you feel drier. Next, you need to screw up your courage—every ounce you can muster—and talk to an adult you trust. If you can't face your mom, pick an aunt, a teacher, a doctor, or a school counselor. It may be hard to imagine now, but talking it out with an adult who has "been there, done that" will make you feel much better.

Left Out

Everybody in my class has become a "woman" and I am still just a "girl." When everyone talks about being "women," I just hang back.

Maxi Pad

It's heartbreaking to feel that your friends are leaving you behind just because their bodies are changing at a different pace than yours. But that doesn't make these girls "women." There's a lot more to being an adult than getting your period and growing breasts. Still, your classmates may be feeling excited about the changes they're going through, maybe even a little afraid. And that's why they need to talk about them so much. Instead of feeling left out, can you listen in? Ask your friends questions about their experiences. You may get firsthand information that will help you when your day comes.

On the Go

Get a leg up on grooming your growing **legs** and protecting your **feet** from pain and odor. Learn how to turn **fitness** into fun, and to practice **sports safety** with the right equipment, exercises, and first-aid basics. And when it's time to **rest,** here's advice on how to get a good night's **sleep** so you can start every day fresh and ready to get into gear!

Legs

Give your legs a hand for all that hard work they do to keep you up and running!

If you think you're ready to start shaving your legs, talk it over with a parent first.

Growing Pains

During puberty, you're going to shoot up in height. Your legs in particular are going to lengthen and grow. For a while, you may feel like your body is all legs. This rapid growth may also cause a tired, achy, cramped feeling in your legs. These occasional *growing pains* usually go away after puberty. And don't worry if your legs seem out of proportion for a while—the rest of you will soon catch up!

And Growing Hair

About the time you start to grow hair under your arms, you may notice that you're sprouting more hair on your legs, too. This hair is usually darker and coarser below the knee than above it. Though there's no real reason to remove leg hair, many girls prefer the look and feel of smooth shins. But once you begin removing leg hair, it may feel coarse and "stubbly" for a time as it grows back, and it may be more noticeable during this phase. So if you start shaving, you'll want to make it a regular part of your grooming routine from now on.

Shave Where?

Most girls shave only the hair on their shins and calves, south of the knees. The hair above the knees is usually so fine that it's not necessary to remove it—and it's an awful lot of leg to shave!

How to Shave

1. You'll need your parent's help to buy a razor with replaceable blades or a supply of disposable razors. Disposable razors are easy to use but good for only a few shaves. A razor with replaceable blades is less wasteful, but changing the blades can be tricky.

2. Get your legs good and wet. You're more likely to nick yourself if your skin and hair aren't thoroughly moistened. Lather on a generous amount of soap or shaving cream or gel.

3. Start at the bottom and pull the razor slowly and gently up your leg with long, smooth strokes. Be careful around your ankles and knees, where it's easy to nick yourself. If you do cut yourself, rinse the cut with cold water, dry it off, and put pressure on it using a tissue until the bleeding stops.

4. Stop to rinse your razor often so it doesn't get clogged with hair. When you're done shaving, rinse the razor before storing it away. Out of courtesy to other family members, rinse out the shower or tub, too.

5. After drying off, apply some lotion to your legs to soothe and moisturize the skin.

Feet

Your feet take a lot of pounding! Don't let foot and toe woes leave you standing on the sidelines.

P.U.! Foot Odor

The best way to deal with foot odor is to prevent it. Don't go sockless when you wear close-toed shoes! Wear clean cotton socks that absorb sweat, with shoes made of natural materials such as leather or canvas that let feet breathe. Fleece boots and footwear made from plastic and other synthetic materials are a recipe for smelly, sweaty feet. To de-stink your shoes, sprinkle baking soda in them and let them sit overnight. Shake out the baking soda—and the smell—in the morning.

Ouch! Blisters

Blisters are sore spots that develop where your shoes rub against your skin. The friction causes the skin to form a bubble, which sometimes pops or tears open. Don't pop the blister yourself. Place a bandage over it to protect it until the skin can heal. You may want to remove the bandage at night to expose the blister to air. This helps speed the healing.

To keep your toes in tip-top condition, give them a little extra attention.

- When you shower or bathe, be sure to scrub between your toes. Use a nailbrush to scour under the nails.

- Trim your toenails regularly after showering or bathing, when the nail is softest and easiest to cut. Use nail clippers to cut straight across. This helps prevent ingrown toenails, which occur when a sharp corner of the nail grows into the skin.

- Give your toes room to wiggle! Never buy shoes that don't fit, no matter how much you like them—you'll be in too much pain to enjoy how you look. Always measure your feet before buying new shoes.

Itchy! Fungus

You don't have to be an athlete to get athlete's foot, a fungus that spreads in damp places where people go barefoot—locker rooms and pools. You can prevent it by wearing flip-flops or shower shoes. If you notice itching and peeling between your toes, you may have a case. It's easy to treat with powders and sprays from the drugstore, with help from a parent. Air also helps athlete's foot go away. At the end of the day, take off your shoes and socks and wash and dry your feet. Then let them air out!

Fitness

Whether it's skating or swimming, kickball or karate, find a fun way to stay fit. Pretty soon you'll forget it's good for you!

Active Girl = Healthy Girl

You already know that eating a balanced diet is essential to good health. But many girls forget that regular exercise is just as important. In addition to helping you look and feel shipshape, exercise strengthens your heart, gives you energy, helps you sleep better, makes your muscles stronger and more flexible, and builds self-confidence. So get up, get out, and get into gear!

How Much Is Enough?

Doctors and fitness experts recommend at least one hour of physical activity every day, with most of this being aerobic exercise. Aerobic exercise is any activity that gets your muscles working with rhythm (like running, jumping rope, biking, dancing) so that it raises your heart rate and speeds up your breathing. You don't have to get your hour of exercise all at once—you can break it up throughout the day. How do you know if your body is working hard enough? Here's a good rule of thumb: when you're exercising or playing, if you're breathing too hard to sing but you can talk fairly easily, you're going at a good pace.

Just remember that whatever type of exercise you choose, don't get too hung up on counting minutes or monitoring your heart rate. The most important thing is to find fun activities that you love and to do them often.

You don't have to be a superjock to stay in shape. Are you lousy at basketball and softball? Give bowling or strolling a try!

It Adds Up

Do you take the escalator when you could climb the stairs? Do you bug your mom for a ride when you're going only a few blocks? A few simple changes to your daily routine can make a difference.

• Ride your bike to the library instead of taking the bus.

• Volunteer for muscle-building chores, such as weeding the garden or raking leaves.

• Play a game of tag with your little sister or brother.

• Take the dog for a long walk.

Sports Safety

Even the best athletes can get injured if they're not careful. Play it smart! These simple strategies will help you stay in the game.

Warm Up, Cool Down

Whether you're hiking, biking, or spiking a volleyball, always take time to stretch out your muscles and prepare them for the work they're about to do. A proper warm-up eases your body into gear and helps prevent muscle pulls and tears. At the end of your workout, cool down with more gentle stretching. This reduces stiffness and soreness the next day.

Wear the Right Gear

You probably already know how important it is to wear your helmet when biking, inline skating, skateboarding, or skiing. But it might not occur to you to wear bright clothes so others can see you coming! And don't head out on skates without elbow, wrist, and knee guards. Other sports may call for a mouth guard or special padding—check with your coach to see what's recommended. Always wear shoes and clothing that fit properly. High-tops that don't fit snugly can lead to twisted ankles. Skates that are too small are an invitation for blisters.

Don't Overdo It

Pay attention to how your body feels while you're exercising or playing a sport. If you are in pain, are getting dizzy or sick to your stomach, or are unable to catch your breath, stop immediately and rest. All of these are warning signs to slo-o-o-w down.

Drink LOTS of Water

When you're active, your body keeps you cool by producing sweat. You need to replace the fluids your body is losing by drinking lots of water before, during, and after you exercise. Fill up a sports bottle before you get going, and refill it often.

Sprain Training

Whether you're a ballet dancer or a soccer goalie, you'll probably deal with injuries from time to time. One of the most common injuries is a sprain, a painful pull or tear in the tissue of a joint that causes the joint to swell up and turn black and blue. Fingers, wrists, elbows, knees, and ankles are easy targets. If you think you've sprained something, the first thing to do is to follow the first-aid rules of R.I.C.E., as shown below. If you are in a lot of pain or not getting better, then get to a doctor as soon as you can to have it checked out.

Rest. Avoid using the sprained joint or putting weight on it.

Ice. Apply an ice pack—or bag of frozen peas or corn—to help shrink swelling and ease the pain.

Compression. Wrap the sprained area snugly in a stretchy sports bandage to keep it stiff and to protect it from further injury.

Elevation. Keep the sprained joint raised on a stack of pillows to help the swelling go down.

Rest

To be healthy, your body needs plenty of rest. Sleep is your body's way of recharging to meet the challenges of each new day.

Good Night!

What's the secret to a sound night's sleep? Develop sound sleeping habits. Getting enough rest helps you look and feel your very best.

Stick to a regular bedtime. One of the best ways to ensure a good night's sleep is to get up and go to bed at the same time every day. If you sleep late one morning, then get up early the next, you may feel tired and groggy all day and have trouble sleeping that night.

Develop a routine. It's a good idea to create a ritual, a special routine, that tells your body it's time to go to sleep. Listen to gentle music, take a warm bath, read a book, or write in a journal. Try to repeat your ritual every night at the same time.

Exercise. Active girls who exercise regularly are often the soundest sleepers of all. Exercise helps release extra energy and tension that can interfere with sleep. But don't exercise too close to bedtime or you may have trouble winding down!

Watch what you drink. Many sodas—especially colas—contain a substance called caffeine that can make you feel jumpy and wide awake. Caffeine is also in coffee, tea, and chocolate. Avoid anything with caffeine at night, especially close to bedtime.

Don't go to bed stuffed. A tummy that's churning because it's too full makes a bad bunkmate. If your stomach is growling from hunger, though, a glass of milk before bedtime is OK.

How Many ZZZs?

Some girls need more sleep than others, but most girls your age need at least ten hours of sleep per night. When your body is growing and changing, you may need more sleep than usual. Aim to get the same amount of sleep each night to give your body consistency—this is the very best way to stay healthy and to grow well. But if you have a few nights in a row of staying up late and you feel exhausted, you may want to try catching up on the weekend by going to bed early, sleeping in, or even napping.

Sleep Troubles

Do you dread going to bed? Is nighttime a nightmare for you? Lots of girls have problems that creep into their sleep.

Bed-Wetting

Wetting the bed is a condition that doctors call *enuresis* (en-yer-EE-sis), and it's more common than you might think. Enuresis usually occurs when a person's bladder is too small to hold all of the urine her body produces in the night. If the sleeper doesn't wake up in time to go to the bathroom, she wets the bed. Almost everyone with this condition outgrows it eventually—and usually if a girl has it, one of her parents did, too. In the meantime, if you're struggling with enuresis, talk to your doctor. There are several treatments you can try—from alarms that help you wake up to prescription medicines that decrease the amount of urine your body produces.

Insomnia

"I've got *insomnia*" is a fancy way of saying "I can't sleep." Insomnia is often caused by having a lot on your mind. You may be so excited or worried about something that you can't stop thinking about it. Insomnia can also be caused by caffeine and other chemicals in certain foods and medicines. Almost everyone has insomnia once in a while, but if you find yourself wide awake night after night, talk to a parent or your doctor. In the meantime, try this relaxation trick. Close your eyes and lie on your back. Then relax your feet, relax your legs, and keep going until you've relaxed every muscle in your body. From head to toe, you'll be ready to go—straight to sleep, that is!

To unwind your mind, try listening to relaxing music or to recordings of soothing sounds from nature.

Nightmares

It's normal to have a bad dream occasionally. Nightmares can seem very realistic, or they can make no sense at all. Either way, they're usually related to something real that's bothering you. If scary dreams invade your sleep every night, talk to your parents or a counselor to help you find out what's on your mind.

Body Talk

It's hard to feel perky in the a.m. when you've got sleep problems that plague you in the p.m.!

Too Worried to Sleep

I have trouble sleeping. I try reading and relaxing before bed. My parents are getting a divorce, but I don't like thinking about it. It hurts! Do you think deep in my mind I think about the divorce and it's keeping me up?

Hurt & Sleepy

Emotional upset and anxiety can definitely cause sleepless nights. Of course you feel scared and sad about your parents' divorce—any girl would. But when your daytime worries start to haunt you at bedtime, you need to do more than toss and turn. You need to get help. Talk to your parents, a teacher, a counselor, or another adult you trust about how much you're hurting. It's hard to have sweet dreams when you've got a heavy heart.

Security Blanket

I am 11 years old and I still sleep with a "blankie." I know a lot of girls do, but definitely not as old as me! Every time I go to a friend's to sleep over, she says stuff like, "Did you bring your security blanket?" and then laughs her head off.

Still sleeping with a "blankie"

Have you considered taking just a piece of your bedtime buddy with you? Cut off a teeny corner of your blanket and pin it inside your sleeping bag—a secret place that only you know about. Or, if you can't bear to cut up your blanket, maybe you can laugh along with your friend. When she asks about the blanket, say with a smile, "You know me, I never leave home without it!" And don't worry, you'll give up your blanket when you're ready.

Bed Wetter

I still wet my bed. My best friend doesn't know and keeps inviting me to slumber parties. She feels sad when I say I can't go. I would really like to sleep over to make my friend happy, but how can I do it without getting embarrassed?

Ashamed

Keeping your bed-wetting a secret only adds to the feeling that it's something shameful—and it's not. If your friend is kind and caring, you may find there's relief in telling her the truth. You can still enjoy sleepovers with your friend by inviting her to your house. If she's having a party, ask if you can go to the first half of the party and have your parents pick you up before bedtime. You'll get to share in most of the fun. You're sure to outgrow bed-wetting eventually. But in the meantime, talk to your doctor about solutions.

Night Fright

I'm afraid of the dark and I can't sleep. What should I do?

afraid

For starters, you need to figure out exactly what it is about the dark that frightens you. Once you've identified what triggers your fright, ask your parents to help you brainstorm ways to banish your fears. Are there things in the room that scare you, such as the dark closet, the curtains flapping in the window, or other objects that cast scary shadows? Try placing a nightlight in your room so that you can see in all of the dark corners. Is it night noises that give you the heebie-jeebies? Investigate the source of the spooky sounds in the light of day. Once you know that *creak-creak* is coming from the furnace and not from phantoms, you're sure to rest easier.

The Girl Inside

Taking care of your **feelings** is just as important as taking care of your body. Find out what to do when oceans of emotions are washing over you, and get tips for **talking it out** with family and friends. Finally, as you get ready to move forward into the future, take a moment to stop and celebrate **the whole you!**

Your Feelings

Mad one minute, sad the next? Feel like you're riding an emotional roller coaster? You're not going crazy; you're just growing up.

It's normal for a growing girl to want a little privacy. Just make sure that when you shut the bedroom door, you don't shut out the people you love. Puberty can be a confusing time, but it doesn't need to be a lonely one. Now more than ever, you need the support of your family.

Ups and Downs

You already know the outside of you will undergo big changes during puberty. But you might not be prepared for so many changes inside of you. During this time, it's normal to experience strong emotions. Don't be surprised if your moods come and go and change like the weather. One minute you're feeling sunny, the next minute stormy. What's behind this flood of laughter and tears? Hormones! The same hormones that tell your body to wake up and grow can strongly affect your feelings, too.

New Directions

As you get older, it's natural for your interests to change. Some of the toys and games you used to love suddenly get pushed to the back of the closet. New interests may take their place. You may also begin to notice boys in a whole different way. That's perfectly OK. There's room in your life for lots of different interests, old and new.

Hang On

It's easy to get caught up in the tide of what other girls are saying and doing. They may even put pressure on you to do as they do. But be careful. It's easy to get lost in the crowd and lose sight of what's right for you. If your friends are going crazy about movie stars and makeup and you'd rather be building a tree fort, don't just cave in and go with the flow. Listen to your heart and be true to you.

Time Out!

Temper tantrums are OK for two-year-olds, who don't know how to control their emotions. But tears and screaming won't get you what you want now that you're older. Part of growing up is learning how to express anger and frustration calmly, in a way that's fair to others.

100

"It's good to talk out problems with the people you have them with." *Ukiah*

Dealing with Feelings

"Forget it. You won't understand."

"You treat me like a baby!"

"I hate you!"

Your whole world is turned topsy-turvy, and there's a tidal wave of emotion crashing around inside of you. You might feel angry, jealous, afraid, embarrassed, or just plain lost and confused. What do you do? If you're like many people, you take it out on the people closest to you. And the trouble with this is that sulky silences and angry outbursts build a wall between people. The wall doesn't go up overnight—it's built one brick at a time. A mean word here. A slammed door there. Before you know it, there's a wall too high for either side to climb over. Don't let this happen to you. Instead of building walls, build bridges by learning to say how you feel in a healthy, helpful way.

Cooling Down

Before you can talk about your feelings, you need to have a calm head. Take a few deep breaths. Take a walk. Take a bath. Write in your journal. Cuddle the dog. Blow off steam, and you'll be less likely to say or do something that you'll regret later. Once you've cooled down, you're ready to talk.

Talking It Out

Telling people how you feel, honestly and calmly, can bring you closer. It shows that you trust them with your feelings. And you open the door for them to share their feelings with you. Besides, talking to others can help you sort out feelings that are confusing you. You need to be able to share anger, fear, and sadness—as well as excitement and happiness—to get the support you need during this challenging time.

Making It Better

Anger can be helpful when it leads to change. For that to happen, you need to try to explain how you feel. Follow these steps to say what's on your mind:

1. Describe exactly what made you angry. "Mom, it made me mad when you said I couldn't have a new swimsuit, right off the bat, without even listening to my reasons for wanting one."

2. Tell how it made you feel. "I felt like you didn't care about my feelings."

3. Try to agree on a way to handle things in the future. "Next time, let's hear each other out before deciding. Maybe together we'll think of a solution that will make us both happy."

The Whole You

Always remember there's more—much more—to you than your body. It's your head, your heart, and your spirit, too, that add up to make YOU.

Your eyes have a unique way of **seeing** the world.

Your head is abuzz with creative ideas, hopes, and **dreams.**

Your ears **listen** to other points of view.

Your voice confidently **expresses** your thoughts and feelings.

Your arms are always ready to **reach** out to others.

Your heart is full of **kindness.**

Your legs **stand up** for what's right.

Your feet are ready to **move ahead** to a bright future!

Write to us!

At American Girl, we love hearing from girls just like you. Tell us what you think of *The Care and Keeping of You.* Send your thoughts and questions to:

The Care and Keeping of You Editor
American Girl
8400 Fairway Place
Middleton, WI 53562

(All comments and suggestions received by American Girl may be used without compensation or acknowledgment. Sorry—photos can't be returned.)

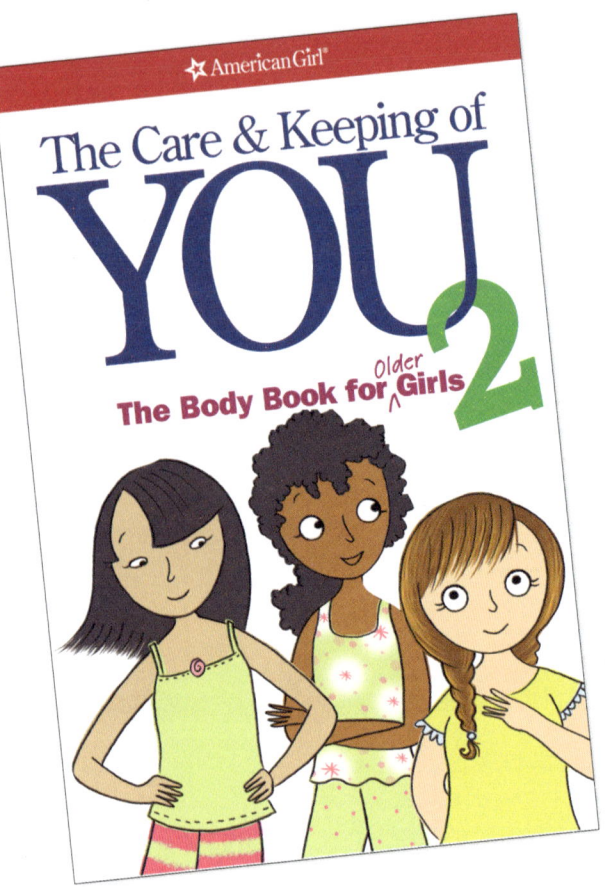

Comfortable with the information you read about in this book? If so, great! Understanding your changing body and feelings is an important part of growing up. What you learned may be enough for now, but soon, as you continue to develop, you may have more questions and need more advice. When you do, *The Care and Keeping of You 2* will be waiting for you!

Here are some other American Girl books you might like:

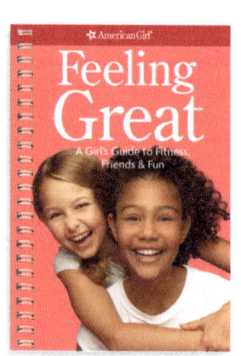

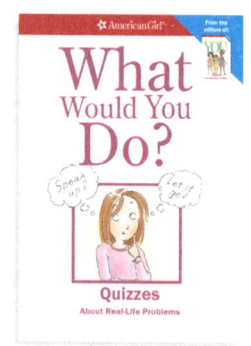

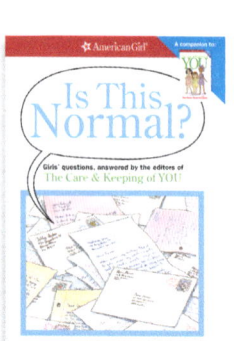

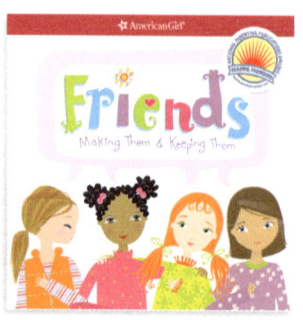